4248   3619

☑ W9-AYM-810

OPPOSING VIEWPOINTS® SERIES

Global Warming

Other Books of Related Interest:

"Congress shall make no law . . . abridging the freedom of speech, or of the press."

First Amendment to the U.S. Constitution

The basic foundation of our democracy is the First Amendment guarantee of freedom of expression. The *Opposing Viewpoints* Series is dedicated to the concept of this basic freedom and the idea that it is more important to practice it than to enshrine it.

OPPOSING VIEWPOINTS® SERIES

Global Warming

David Haugen, Susan Musser, and Kacy Lovelace,
Book Editors

GREENHAVEN PRESS
A part of Gale, Cengage Learning

GALE
CENGAGE Learning™

Detroit • New York • San Francisco • New Haven, Conn • Waterville, Maine • London

GALE
CENGAGE Learning

Christine Nasso, *Publisher*
Elizabeth Des Chenes, *Managing Editor*

© 2010 Greenhaven Press, a part of Gale, Cengage Learning.

Gale and Greenhaven Press are registered trademarks used herein under license.

For more information, contact:
Greenhaven Press
27500 Drake Rd.
Farmington Hills, MI 48331-3535
Or you can visit our Internet site at gale.cengage.com

For product information and technology assistance, contact us at

Gale Customer Support, 1-800-877-4253
For permission to use material from this text or product, submit all requests online at
www.cengage.com/permissions

Further permissions questions can be emailed to permissionrequest@cengage.com

Articles in Greenhaven Press anthologies are often edited for length to meet page requirements. In addition, original titles of these works are changed to clearly present the main thesis and to explicitly indicate the author's opinion. Every effort is made to ensure that Greenhaven Press accurately reflects the original intent of the authors. Every effort has been made to trace the owners of copyrighted material.

Image copyright Andrejs Pidjass, 2009. Used under license from Shutterstock.com

LIBRARY OF CONGRESS CATALOGING-IN-PUBLICATION DATA

Global warming / David Haugen, Susan Musser, and Kacy Lovelace, book editors.
    p. cm. -- (Opposing viewpoints)
    Includes bibliographical references and index.
    978-0-7377-4631-0 (hardcover) -- ISBN 978-0-7377-4632-7 (pbk.)
    1. Global warming. I. Haugen, David, 1969- II. Musser, Susan. III. Lovelace, Kacy.
    QC981.8.G56G578 2010
    363.738'74--dc22
                                                            2009038723

Printed in the United States of America
1 2 3 4 5 6 7 13 12 11 10 09

Contents

Chapter 3: What Is the Impact of Global Warming?

Why Consider Opposing Viewpoints?

> *"The only way in which a human being can make some approach to knowing the whole of a subject is by hearing what can be said about it by persons of every variety of opinion and studying all modes in which it can be looked at by every character of mind. No wise man ever acquired his wisdom in any mode but this."*
>
> John Stuart Mill

In our media-intensive culture it is not difficult to find differing opinions. Thousands of newspapers and magazines and dozens of radio and television talk shows resound with differing points of view. The difficulty lies in deciding which opinion to agree with and which "experts" seem the most credible. The more inundated we become with differing opinions and claims, the more essential it is to hone critical reading and thinking skills to evaluate these ideas. *Opposing Viewpoints* books address this problem directly by presenting stimulating debates that can be used to enhance and teach these skills. The varied opinions contained in each book examine many different aspects of a single issue. While examining these conveniently edited opposing views, readers can develop critical thinking skills such as the ability to compare and contrast authors' credibility, facts, argumentation styles, use of persuasive techniques, and other stylistic tools. In short, the *Opposing Viewpoints* Series is an ideal way to attain the higher-level thinking and reading skills so essential in a culture of diverse and contradictory opinions.

In addition to providing a tool for critical thinking, *Opposing Viewpoints* books challenge readers to question their own strongly held opinions and assumptions. Most people form their opinions on the basis of upbringing, peer pressure, and personal, cultural, or professional bias. By reading carefully balanced opposing views, readers must directly confront new ideas as well as the opinions of those with whom they disagree. This is not to simplistically argue that everyone who reads opposing views will—or should—change his or her opinion. Instead, the series enhances readers' understanding of their own views by encouraging confrontation with opposing ideas. Careful examination of others' views can lead to the readers' understanding of the logical inconsistencies in their own opinions, perspective on why they hold an opinion, and the consideration of the possibility that their opinion requires further evaluation.

Evaluating Other Opinions

To ensure that this type of examination occurs, *Opposing Viewpoints* books present all types of opinions. Prominent spokespeople on different sides of each issue as well as well-known professionals from many disciplines challenge the reader. An additional goal of the series is to provide a forum for other, less known, or even unpopular viewpoints. The opinion of an ordinary person who has had to make the decision to cut off life support from a terminally ill relative, for example, may be just as valuable and provide just as much insight as a medical ethicist's professional opinion. The editors have two additional purposes in including these less known views. One, the editors encourage readers to respect others' opinions—even when not enhanced by professional credibility. It is only by reading or listening to and objectively evaluating others' ideas that one can determine whether they are worthy of consideration. Two, the inclusion of such viewpoints encourages the important critical thinking skill of objectively evaluating an author's credentials and bias. This evaluation will illuminate an author's reasons for taking a particular stance on an issue and will aid in readers' evaluation of the author's ideas.

It is our hope that these books will give readers a deeper understanding of the issues debated and an appreciation of the complexity of even seemingly simple issues when good and honest people disagree. This awareness is particularly important in a democratic society such as ours in which people enter into public debate to determine the common good. Those with whom one disagrees should not be regarded as enemies but rather as people whose views deserve careful examination and may shed light on one's own.

Thomas Jefferson once said that "difference of opinion leads to inquiry, and inquiry to truth." Jefferson, a broadly educated man, argued that "if a nation expects to be ignorant and free . . . it expects what never was and never will be." As individuals and as a nation, it is imperative that we consider the opinions of others and examine them with skill and discernment. The *Opposing Viewpoints* Series is intended to help readers achieve this goal.

David L. Bender and Bruno Leone,
Founders

Introduction

"An honest, objective assessment of the present state of knowledge about climate change is that while we do know quite a lot, we cannot be sure that we are aware of everything that could possibly happen, given the complexity of the planet's meteorological system and ecology. We cannot even be certain of our ability to unambiguously calculate the chances [of] the outcomes we do know about. When it comes down to it, much that we would like to know to understand the details of the climate change problem more precisely is still beyond the boundary of what we now do know."

Lloyd J. Dumas,
"Seeds of Opportunity:
Climate Change Challenges
and Solutions," April 2006.

Swedish physicist Svante Arrhenius was the first scientist to assert that heightened concentrations of carbon dioxide in the atmosphere could lead to global warming. In 1896 Arrhenius—using the notion of a greenhouse effect proposed by previous investigators—put forth his theory that increases in the amount of carbon dioxide in the atmosphere would result in an arithmetic rise in the temperature of the earth. He predicted that if the amount of carbon dioxide emissions was doubled from their late nineteenth-century levels, the surface of the planet would heat up five degrees Celsius. Because he was initially interested in explaining the causes of the ice ages that had so plagued humanity in the past, Arrhenius believed that such an increase in temperature might be a boon for humankind. Still, Arrhenius expected that it would take roughly three millennia before carbon concentrations reached the level needed to bring about the 5 degree change.

Arrhenius's work was criticized in his time, and because most scientists believed that the weather was affected more by solar cycles and other natural forces than by the insignificant contributions of humans, the science of global warming was largely ignored for decades. Declining global temperatures through the mid-twentieth century also made many fear that the world was headed for another ice age. But in the 1980s the trend in temperature curves began to turn. In 1988 measurements showed that the planet was warmer than it had been in any period over the past 100 years, and the United Nations formed the Intergovernmental Panel on Climate Change (IPCC) to publish reports on climate change and its possible harmful effects. Two years later the IPCC released its first report, claiming that carbon dioxide emissions were chiefly responsible for enhancing the greenhouse effect. The panel also concluded that the result of this had been a global warming of 0.3–0.6 degrees Celsius since 1880, suggesting that the rise in temperatures was occurring much faster than Arrhenius forecasted. IPCC reports in 1992, 1995, and 2001 supported these conclusions and also drew a clear connection between global warming and human-produced greenhouse emissions.

The IPCC findings, however, have not convinced every scientist or interested observer that global warming is happening or that human pollution is responsible for climate change. S. Fred Singer, a professor emeritus and atmospheric physicist at the University of Virginia, was one of 500 scientists who attended a conference of skeptics in 2008 that reexamined the peer-reviewed studies that informed the IPCC's reports. As Singer stated, "We reached the opposite conclusion" than the IPCC, asserting instead that climate change was a result of mainly natural causes such as changes in the sun's energy output. Singer told the *Washington Post* that human-made greenhouse emissions were therefore "not a cause for concern, at least not yet." Some skeptics still contend that because current weather patterns reveal record cold spells, the world may simply be fluctuating in and out of warm and chilly periods as it has done cyclically for centuries. Senator James Inhofe of Oklahoma claims that the media spin these natural cycles into coming cataclysms. "Since 1895," Inhofe told the Senate in 2006, "the media has alternated between global cooling and warming scares during four separate and sometimes overlapping time periods." Having referred to global warming as "the greatest hoax ever perpetrated on the American people," Inhofe warned Congress that "breaking the cycles of media hysteria will not be easy since hysteria sells."

Those who insist that global warming is a real and dire phenomenon maintain that facts, not hype, compel the world's attention. "The science is screaming at us," U.S. senator John Kerry of Massachusetts told the Senate Foreign Relations Committee in January 2009. At the same meeting, former U.S. Vice President Al Gore claimed, "More and more Americans are paying attention to the new evidence and fresh warnings from scientists," indicating that there was a growing consensus that climate change is an undeniable and dangerous threat. Just over a year previously, Gore had made a similar statement: "The experts have told us [global warming] is not a passing affliction that will heal by itself. We asked for a second opinion. And a third. And a fourth. And the consistent conclusion, restated with increasing alarm, is that something basic is wrong. We are what is wrong, and we must make it right."

Though other nations have pledged to "make it right," it is still uncertain whether the United States will act to redress climate change and its potential hazards. The American Senate never had a chance to ratify the Kyoto Protocol, an international agreement approved by 183 governments to reduce greenhouse gas emissions, even though then–vice president Al

Gore did sign the treaty. Different bureaus of the U.S. government proffered different claims on whether America's economy would suffer by adopting the protocol, and Gore was one of many who believed the treaty would not work if—as it was written—developing nations were not compelled to do their share of reducing emissions. Foreign allies, especially those of the European Union, have criticized America's ratification refusal as a sign that the country—now the second largest producer of greenhouse gases—lacks the courage or will to face its global responsibilities.

At the outset of the presidential administration of Barack Obama, America's stance on the Kyoto Protocol is still noncommittal. However, Obama's words in his presidential campaign and his initial days in office have given many environmentalists hope that his administration will steer a clear path towards energy efficiency, the reduction of greenhouse emissions, and cooperation with global partners. In a taped statement to a Governors Global Climate Summit in Los Angeles, California, in November 2008, the then president-elect asserted:

> Few challenges facing America—and the world—are more urgent than combating climate change. The science is beyond dispute and the facts are clear. Sea levels are rising. Coastlines are shrinking. We've seen record drought, spreading famine, and storms that are growing stronger with each passing hurricane season . . . My presidency will mark a new chapter in America's leadership on climate change that will strengthen our security and create millions of new jobs in the process.

According to Obama, his administration will implement a cap-and-trade system for carbon emissions to compel industries to reduce pollutants to 1990 levels by 2020, and he intends to invest $15 billion per year in clean coal technologies as well as solar power, wind power, and biofuels. In the same announcement, Obama pledged to world leaders that "once I take office, you can be sure that the United States will once again engage vigorously in [international] negotiations, and help lead the world toward a new era of global cooperation on climate change."

Such promises may please those who believe change is needed, but these pronouncements still worry those who contend that the science is unproven and that an uncompromising shift toward "greening" America could destabilize the economy of the nation and the world. As this anthology, *Opposing Viewpoints: Global Warming*, illustrates, the issues surrounding climate change are unsettled and contentious. In chapters that ask, Is Global Warming a Real Phenomenon? What Causes Global Warming? What Is the Impact of Global Warming? and How Can Global Warming Be Mitigated? politicians, climate experts, and other observers offer differing perspectives that bespeak concerns for the environment, the economy, national security, and individual liberties in addressing climate change. While some may dismiss the reality of global warming entirely, most are anxious to see that America and the world act wisely in choosing appropriate policies that are practical, efficient, and based on reasoned scientific conclusions.

OPPOSING VIEWPOINTS® SERIES

CHAPTER 1

Is Global Warming a Real Phenomenon?

Chapter Preface

According to NASA's Goddard Institute for Space Studies, the average global temperature in the 1970s was 14.01 degrees Celsius. Over the next two decades, the average global temperatures rose to 14.40 degrees Celsius, and in the first five years of the new millennium, this number has increased to 14.59 degrees Celsius. Indeed, the eight hottest years on record—a record that has been kept since 1880—have all occurred within the decade spanning from 1998–2008. The Intergovernmental Panel on Climate Change (IPCC), a collective of 1,250 scientists from various countries, predicts that given current trends, the world can expect temperatures to continue to go up in the twenty-first century by anywhere from 1.1 to 6.4 degrees Celsius.

The IPCC and many other climatologists claim the warming of the planet is being caused by the release of chiefly human-made greenhouse gases into the atmosphere. Since the Industrial Revolution, the amount of carbon dioxide and other gases spewed from factories has increased, but more recently power plants and the advent of the automobile have added to a precipitous climb in emissions. In its 2007 climate report, the IPCC boldly stated, "Most of the observed increase in globally averaged temperatures since the mid-20th century is very likely due to the observed increase in anthropogenic greenhouse gas concentrations." Some believe that the trend is so distinct a phenomenon that a new planetary epoch—the Anthropocene Age—has arrived to denote this period in which global climate is primarily dictated by human activity.

Other observers are less certain of the connection between human-made greenhouse gas emissions and the rise in temperatures. Stephen Wilde, a fellow of the Royal Meteorological Society in London, points out that the steady rise in carbon dioxide evident since the 1950s has not corresponded with a steady rise in global temperatures. "Instead we see rises and falls in global temperatures that bear no obvious relationship to the steady rise in CO_2," he writes, "unless one puts the cart before the horse and announces that there is no other possible reason and the trend period adopted is carefully chosen to suit the proposition." He implies that the rising temperatures might be the earth recovering from the Little Ice Age that began in the 1600s. "On a balance of probability, is that not the more likely explanation of an overall warming trend ever since? Why introduce manmade CO_2 at all except for politically motivated reasons?" he adds.

Whether the warming trend evident in recent decades corresponds to greenhouse emissions is the topic taken up by the authors in the following chapter. Some warn of a coming global climate crisis, while others assert that temperature change is a natural part of the planet's climate cycles. Deroy Murdock even offers evidence that the world might be cooling, not warming, suggesting that the Little Ice Age may not have yet released the globe from its grip.

> "It may be hardly noticeable to most of us, but the world's temperature is rising."

Global Warming Is Real

Ben Bova

In the following viewpoint, prolific science fiction author Ben Bova claims that global warming is a real phenomenon. Dismissing the opinions of naysayers, Bova contends that measurable scientific facts show that temperatures on the planet are rising and that human-produced greenhouse gases are the culprit for the changes in the weather. Bova fears that the earth will experience a shift toward a tropical climate in a few decades unless people and governments act to redress the problem.

As you read, consider the following questions:

1. On what part of the earth does Bova say rising temperatures are most notable?

2. How does Bova use the research survey at Yosemite National Park to show evidence of global warming?

3. Why does Bova believe that doubters are hostile to the idea that humans are causing global warming?

I have a number of friends who don't believe that global warming is real. They suspect it's all a plot by Third World collectivist nations to cripple our economy.

Global warming has lots of doubters.

For example, in a commencement address a couple of years ago, the late author Michael Crichton remarked that if weather forecasts can't be depended on for accurate predictions a few days ahead, why should we take seriously alarms about a global warming that won't fully manifest itself until decades or even centuries from now?

Global-warming opponents are quick to jump on any shred of evidence that the current warming trend isn't global, or is not actually happening. They have long pointed out that as recently as the 1970s climate experts believed that the Earth was cooling, not warming.

NASA's Goddard Institute for Space Studies, one of the main sources for global-warming data, was embarrassed recently when it had to admit that its declaration that last month [2008] was the warmest October on record was wrong, based on a faulty reading of the temperatures in Siberia.

One of my closest friends sent me through the Internet a newspaper account of the Goddard fiasco, together with 136 pages of comments by various bloggers, many of them gloating over the error.

Get the Facts

In the face of such doubts and mistakes, though, I remembered a piece of wisdom uttered by the great science-fiction writer Robert A. Heinlein. A graduate of the U.S. Naval Academy, Heinlein once told a graduating class at Annapolis:

What are the facts? Again and again and again—what are the facts? Shun wishful thinking, ignore divine revelation, forget "what the stars foretell," avoid opinion, care not for what the neighbors think, never mind the unguessable "ver-

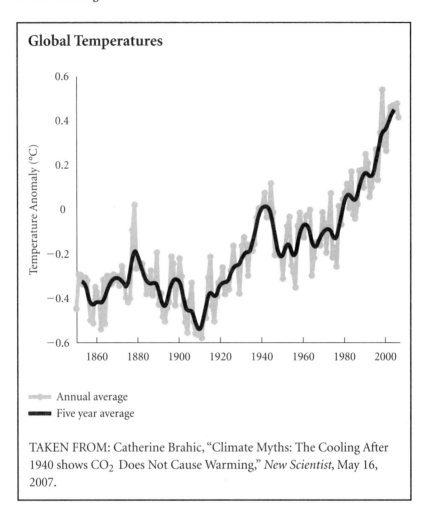

Global Temperatures

Temperature Anomaly (°C)

▬▬ Annual average
▬▬ Five year average

TAKEN FROM: Catherine Brahic, "Climate Myths: The Cooling After 1940 shows CO_2 Does Not Cause Warming," *New Scientist*, May 16, 2007.

dict of history"—what are the facts, and to how many decimal places? You pilot always into an unknown future; facts are your single clue. Get the facts!

The facts are based on actual temperature measurements around the world. Despite the Goddard Institute's recent gaffe, those measurements consistently show that global temperatures are rising. The rise is most noticeable at high latitudes, where Canadian and Siberian villages that have for centuries rested on solid ground are now sinking into mud, because the permafrost beneath them is thawing.

Migrating animals head north earlier because spring temperatures are arriving weeks earlier in the year. Plants blossom earlier too. And both plant and animal species are expanding their habitats northward because of the generally warmer temperatures. Arctic sea ice is thinning drastically. Glaciers are melting away.

These are observable, measurable facts.

The Planet Is Certainly Not Cooling

In California's Yosemite National Park, a group of researchers recently completed a survey of small mammals in an area that had been surveyed about a century earlier by other scientists. The new survey found that, compared to a century ago, species that lived at low altitudes have moved their habitats to higher areas, while the original high-altitude species have declined in numbers. This is a clear response to a warming climate: as the climate heats up, the low-altitude species are seeking cooler habitats and making inroads on the living space of the original high-altitude species.

Field mice and pine trees don't have politics. They are responding to the climate changes that they face. Those changes are real.

What's not real is the claim that until the 1970s climate scientists were worried about Earth's climate cooling into a new ice age. That's a canard. A team from the National Climatic Data Center in North Carolina surveyed climate research papers published between 1965 and 1979; their study showed that only seven papers predicted that global temperatures would grow cooler, while 44 papers predicted warmer temperatures and another 20 were either neutral or offered no long-term predictions.

Humans Are at Fault

The climate-change doubters are especially hostile to the idea that human actions are causing global warming. They fear that attempts to control climate-altering greenhouse-gas emissions are thinly-disguised attacks on the economies of the Western nations, especially the economy of the United States.

While I agree that the Kyoto Treaty's approach to lowering greenhouse-gas emissions is a half-baked piece of international politics, and the U.S. is right to refuse to sign it, it seems equally clear to me that human actions are indeed causing at least part of the planet's rising fever.

Our Earth goes through climate shifts over the course of time, but the greenhouse gases we humans are pouring into the atmosphere are accelerating a natural warming trend. If we can move away from fossil fuels without doing fatal harm to our economy and our way of life, it will alleviate the warming.

In his famous "Liberty or Death" speech, Patrick Henry said, ". . . it is natural to man to indulge in the illusions of hope. . . . Are we disposed to be of the number of those who, having eyes, see not, and having ears, hear not, the things which so nearly concern their temporal salvation? For my part, whatever anguish of spirit it may cost, I am willing to know the whole truth; to know the worst and to provide for it."

Despite the naysayers, global warming is real. It may be hardly noticeable to most of us, but the world's temperature is rising. How far and how fast it will rise, no one can yet predict. But studies of past climate changes show that the planet can switch from ice age to tropical in a few decades.

If we want to avert wrenching changes that would come with an accelerated global warming, we should do all we could to move from fossil fuels to cleaner, less-damaging energy sources. Such a change would be good not only for our global climate, but it would be good for our economy and the world's political situation, as well.

Look at the facts. Make up your mind. Then act.

> *"In the last 1.6 million years there have been 63 alternations between warm and cold climates, and no indication that any of them were caused by changes in carbon dioxide levels."*

Global Warming Is a Myth

Edmund Contoski

Edmund Contoski is a retired environmental consultant who now serves as a columnist for FORCES International Liberty News Network, an organization that advocates individual liberty unfettered by state-imposed restrictions. In the following viewpoint, Contoski asserts that global warming is scientifically unproven and that the facts reveal that the earth periodically experiences changing climates. He denies that carbon dioxide emissions have any noticeable impact on global temperatures and furthermore claims that human-made emissions are insignificant when compared to the carbon output of natural sources that have always been beyond human control.

As you read, consider the following questions:

1. Why does Contoski argue that carbon dioxide is the weakest of greenhouse gases?

Edmund Contoski, "Global Warming, Global Myth," *Liberty*, vol. 22, September 2008. © Copyright 2008, Liberty Foundation. Reproduced by permission.

2. What benefits does the author see in warming global temperatures?

3. What hidden political agenda might reside behind global warming alarmism, according to Constoski?

During the 20th century, the earth warmed 0.6 degree Celsius (1 degree Fahrenheit), but that warming has been wiped out in a single year with a drop of 0.63 degree C. (1.13 F.) in 2007. A single year does not constitute a trend reversal, but the magnitude of that temperature drop—equal to 100 years of warming—is noteworthy. Of course, it can also be argued that a mere 0.6 degree warming in a century is so tiny it should never have been considered a cause for alarm in the first place. But then how could the idea of global warming be sold to the public? In any case, global cooling has been evident for more than a single year. Global temperature has declined since 1998. Meanwhile, atmospheric carbon dioxide has gone in the other direction, increasing 15–20%. This divergence casts doubt on the validity of the greenhouse hypothesis, but that hasn't discouraged the global warming advocates. They have long been ignoring far greater evidence that the basic assumption of greenhouse warming from increases in carbon dioxide is false.

No Connection Between Carbon Dioxide and Global Warming

Manmade emissions of carbon dioxide were not significant before worldwide industrialization began in the 1940s. They have increased steadily since. Over 80% of the 20th century's carbon dioxide increase occurred after 1940—but most of the century's temperature increase occurred before 1940! From 1940 until the mid-1970s, the climate also failed to behave according to the greenhouse hypothesis, as carbon dioxide was strongly increasing while global temperatures cooled. This cooling led to countless scare stories in the media about a new ice age commencing.

In the last 1.6 million years there have been 63 alternations between warm and cold climates, and no indication that any of them were caused by changes in carbon dioxide levels. A recent study of a much longer period (600 million years) shows—without exception—that temperature changes precede changes in carbon dioxide levels, not the other way around. As the earth warms, the oceans yield more carbon dioxide to the atmosphere, because warmer water cannot hold as much carbon dioxide as colder water.

The public has been led to believe that increased carbon dioxide from human activities is causing a greenhouse effect that is heating the planet. But carbon dioxide comprises only 0.035% of our atmosphere and is a very weak greenhouse gas. Although it is widely blamed for greenhouse warming, it is not the only greenhouse gas, or even the most important. Water vapor is a strong greenhouse gas and accounts for at least 95% of any greenhouse effect. Carbon dioxide accounts for only about 3%, with the remainder due to methane and several other gases.

Humankind's Carbon Output Is Miniscule

Not only is carbon dioxide's total greenhouse effect puny, mankind's contribution to it is minuscule. The overwhelming majority (97%) of carbon dioxide in the earth's atmosphere comes from nature, not from man. Volcanoes, swamps, rice paddies, fallen leaves, and even insects and bacteria produce carbon dioxide, as well as methane. According to the journal *Science* (Nov. 5, 1982), termites alone emit ten times more carbon dioxide than all the factories and automobiles in the world. Natural wetlands emit more greenhouse gases than all human activities combined. (If greenhouse warming is such a problem, why are we trying to save all the wetlands?) Geothermal activity in Yellowstone National Park emits ten times the carbon dioxide of a midsized coal-burning power plant, and volcanoes emit hundreds of times more. In fact, our atmosphere's composition is primarily the result of volcanic activity. There are about 100 active volcanoes today, mostly in remote locations, and we're living in a period of relatively low volcanic activity. There have been times when volcanic activity was ten times greater than in modern times. But by far the largest source of carbon dioxide emissions is the equatorial Pacific Ocean. It produces 72% of the earth's emissions of carbon dioxide, and the rest of the Pacific, the Atlantic, the Indian Ocean, and the other oceans also contribute. The human contribution is overshadowed by these far larger sources of carbon dioxide. Combining the factors of water vapor and nature's production of carbon dioxide, we see that 99.8% of any greenhouse effect has nothing to do with carbon dioxide emissions from human activity. So how much effect could regulating the tiny remainder have upon world climate, even if carbon dioxide determined climate? . . .

The Benefits of Warming

The global warming advocates make all sorts of false claims about dire consequences of global warming. They claim it will result in the spread of malaria, food shortages, more human deaths, more violent weather, and a loss of biological diversity through the extinction of species. All untrue. The largest number of species—the greatest biological diversity—is in the tropics. As you move away from the equator, you find fewer and fewer species, until you reach the earth's poles, where there is zero diversity because nothing can live there.

Agricultural productivity is also reduced by cold climate, not a warmer one. That's why Siberia and Alaska are not noted for agricultural abundance. A warmer climate would mean longer growing seasons and would make agriculture possible in areas where it isn't today. And there are at least 300 studies showing plants and forests grow faster and more luxuriantly under conditions of increased carbon dioxide.

Where Is the Warming?

There is no significant man made global warming. There has not been any in the past, there is none now and there is no reason to fear any in the future. The climate of Earth is changing. It has always changed. But mankind's activities have not overwhelmed or significantly modified the natural forces.

Through all history, Earth has shifted between two basic climate regimes: ice ages and what paleoclimatologists call "Interglacial periods." For the past 10 thousand years the Earth has been in an interglacial period. . . . Clearly from our point of view, an interglacial period is greatly preferred to the deadly rigors of an ice age. [Former vice president and environmentalist Al] Gore and his crowd would have us believe that the activities of man have overwhelmed nature during this interglacial period and are producing an unprecedented, out of control warming.

Well, it is simply not happening. Worldwide there was a significant natural warming trend in the 1980's and 1990's as a solar cycle peaked with lots of sunspots and solar flares. That ended in 1998 and now the sun has gone quiet with fewer and fewer sun spots, and the global temperatures have gone into decline. Earth has cooled for almost ten straight years. So, I ask Al Gore, where's the global warming?

John Coleman,
Global Warming and the Price of a Gallon of Gas, *2008.*

Our bodies require heat. We are warm-blooded and have no fur. We wear clothes, build homes, and heat them with fires, all as protection against the cold. Far more people move to Florida, California, or Arizona because of warm climate than move to Alaska, North Dakota, or Montana. Canada is the world's second largest country, but 90% of the population lives within 100 miles of its southern border. Worldwide, far more people die every year from cold than from heat. So why should global warming be bad for us? . . .

Contrary Evidence

Here's an example of the global warming alarmists completely ignoring contrary data, or even denying it exists. Some scientists assert that the current level of carbon dioxide in the atmosphere (about 380 parts per million) is the highest in 800,000 years. The media sucks this up and broadcasts it all over the airwaves and the newspapers, and the public, not knowing any better, believes it must be true. But how could such learned men be so ignorant in their own field of expertise as to not know of the abundant temperature records that give lie to their claim? How could they not know of the monumental compilation by Ernst-Georg Beck of more than 90,000 direct carbon dioxide measurements, between 1812 and 1961, from 175 published technical papers? Zbigniew Jaworowski, M.D., Ph.D., D.Sc., says these measurements were ignored for three decades "not because they were wrong. Indeed, these measurements were made by top scientists, including two Nobel Prize winners, using techniques that are standard textbook procedures. . . . The only reason for rejection was that these measurements did not fit the hypothesis of anthropogenic global warming. I regard this as perhaps the greatest scientific scandal of our time." . . .

Why is it that the global warming advocates are unfazed by any contrary evidence, no matter how strong? All their claims of disasters from global warming have been debunked. All their computer models have been shown to be false, to be based on flawed assumptions, incapable of being reconciled with the observable facts. Vaclav Klaus, President of the Czech

Republic and a university professor before he became president, is the author of a book on global warming and has spoken often on the subject. He says, "What frustrates me is the feeling that everything has already been said and published, that all rational argument has been used, yet it does not help." It does not help because global warming alarmism is not based on rational argument. It is not based on science. It is not based on reality. It is based on political ideology. If rational argument doesn't fit, then phony arguments must be invented: the spread of malaria, the loss of biological diversity, polar bears disappearing, etc. If computer models can predict disaster scenarios only by programming unrealistic assumptions, then that will be done. If global warming does not fit the observable temperature measurements, then a new "reality" must be invented to fit the ideology: the actual temperature records must be altered or dismissed. The global warming advocates are not disturbed by all this because, in their view, ideology trumps reality.

Hidden Political Agenda

Patrick Moore, a cofounder and director of Greenpeace, resigned because of its "trend toward abandoning scientific objectivity in favor of political agendas." After the failure of communism, he says, there was little public support for collectivist ideology. In his view, a "reason environmental extremism emerged was because world communism failed, the [Berlin] wall came down, and a lot of peaceniks and political activists moved into the environmental movement bringing their neo-Marxism with them and learned to use green language in a very clever way to cloak agendas that actually have more to do with anticapitalism and antiglobalism than they do anything with ecology or science." . . .

Do you ever wonder how communism could last for 70 years in Russia? Surely there was plenty of evidence, for decades, that the system was failing: food shortages, declining life expectancy, increased infant mortality, low standards of living, primitive hospitals, and sanitation facilities lagging far behind those in Western Europe and America—not to mention pollution far worse than in the West. But to diehard communists, the facts did not matter. All the observable negatives of collectivism were trumped by ideology. The same is true of the ideology behind global warming.

| *"There's great gobs of money to be made from the sale of the climate change snake-oil remedies."*

Global Warming Is a Get-Rich Scam

Michael Reagan

Conservative radio personality Michael Reagan—the eldest son of former U.S. President Ronald Reagan—argues in the following viewpoint that global warming hysteria is a scam that preys on public trust and both public and private finances. According to Reagan, politicians are using unfounded concerns over global warming to raise taxes and to invest tax money into pet projects of no proven value. He also asserts that some environmental scientists are global warming alarmists because they reap the monetary benefits afforded by public and private funding. In Reagan's view, global warming is nothing but a fraud to bilk Americans.

As you read, consider the following questions:

1. As Reagan quotes, what does the Associated Press (AP) say would experience an increase in costs if a carbon tax were enacted?

Michael Reagan, "It's All About Green . . . ," *FrontPageMagazine.com*, October 1, 2007. Reproduced by permission.

2. What did Representative Adam B. Schiff of California get $500,000 to fund, as Reagan reports?

3. According to Reagan, to whom is JunkScience.com's Steven Malloy promising to award $125,000?

Those wonderful folks in Congress who say the world is about to be roasted on the global warming spit have some great ideas on how to stop Mother Nature from barbecuing us and they even have plans on how to pay for the weapons against climate change.

They'll make you pay for it while they get rich.

Forget the fact that the whole man-made global warming theory is a gigantic scam with not a shred of genuine scientific evidence to prove it. Instead, follow the money trail to get an idea of what it's all about. And what it's all about is money—the big bucks the disciples of [former vice president and environmentalist] Al Gore will rake in, and the big bucks you'll have to pay to finance this incredible con game.

Causing Pain to Consumers

Democrat Rep. John Dingell of Michigan, chairman of the House Energy and Commerce Committee, let the cat out of the bag . . . when he told the American people: "I'm trying to have everybody understand that this is going to cost and that it's going to have a measure of pain that you're not going to like."

Dingell's bottom line: "This is going to cause pain."

Among his proposals according to the Associated Press (AP):

A 50-cent-a-gallon tax on gasoline and jet fuel—phased in over five years—on top of existing taxes.

A tax on carbon, at $50 a ton, released from burning coal, petroleum or natural gas. The AP notes that a carbon tax would boost the cost of everything from the cost of electricity to winter heating and gasoline and other motor fuels. Econo-

The Riches of Hysteria

Americans willing to look at the manmade global warming debate with any degree of impartiality and honesty are well aware that those spreading the hysteria have made a lot of money doing so, and stand to gain much more if governments mandate carbon dioxide emissions reductions.

In fact, [in June 2007], ABC News.com estimated soon-to-be-Nobel Laureate Al Gore's net worth at $100 million, which isn't bad considering that he was supposedly worth about $1 million when he watched George W. Bush get sworn in as president in January 2001.

Talk about your get-rich-quick schemes, how'd you like to increase your net worth 10,000 percent in less than seven years?

Noel Sheppard,
"Al Gore Getting Rich Spreading
Global Warming Hysteria with Media's Help,"
News Busters, October 3, 2007. www.newsbusters.org

mists say a cap on carbon also would raise these costs as burning fossil fuels becomes more expensive.

Phase-out of the interest tax deduction on home mortgages for homes over 3,000 square feet. Owners would keep most of the deduction for homes at the lower end of the scale, but it would be eliminated entirely for homes of 4,200 feet or more.

He estimates that would affect 10 percent of homeowners. He says "it's only fair" to tax those who dare to buy large suburban houses and create urban sprawl. People, I might add, such as Al Gore and John Edwards who occupy palatial mansions amongst leafy glades.

Selling Hysteria

Why such punitive measures? As Walter Williams wrote in . . . *Investor's Business Daily* . . . : "Despite increasing evidence that man-made CO_2 is not a significant greenhouse gas and contributor to climate change, politicians and others who wish to control our lives must maintain that it is."

The reason? There's great gobs of money to be made from the sale of the climate change snake-oil remedies.

Al Gore, for example, has become a multi-millionaire selling his brand of snake oil. Big business is lining up to get its share of your tax money extorted from you to pay to fight a non-existent threat, members of Congress are getting ready to legislate anti–climate-change programs to fund projects in their districts, and scientists are living off huge grants to study global warming.

According to Williams, buying into the global warming hysteria allows politicians to do just about anything, upon which they can muster a majority vote, in the name of fighting climate change as a means to raise taxes.

Going After Big Money

He cites Rep. David L. Hobson, R-Ohio, who has already secured $500,000 for a geothermal demonstration project and Rep. Adam B. Schiff, D-Calif., who got $500,000 for a fuel-cell project by Superprotonic, a Pasadena company started by Caltech scientists. Money for similar boondoggles is being called for by members of both parties.

Then there's NASA's hysterical James Hanson, the media's favorite climate change alarmist who Williams reveals was financed by ultra lefty George Soros. Wrote Williams: "James Hansen, a man billed as a lonely 'NASA whistleblower' standing up to the mighty U.S. Government, was really funded by Soros' Open Society Institute, which gave him 'legal and media advice.' That's right, Hansen was packaged for the media by Soros' flagship 'philanthropy,' to the tune of $720,000."

Ironically, in their headlong rush to get their hands on some of the snake-oil money, the climate change hucksters are passing up a chance to get their hands on a cool $125,000.

In their Ultimate Global Warming challenge, Steven Malloy's JunkScience.com says $125,000 will be awarded to the first person to prove, in a scientific manner, that humans are causing harmful global warming.

The challenge has gone unanswered for the last 52 days [as of October 1, 2007].

"*Sometimes there is a knowing authoritarianism in green activism.*"

The Media Are Silencing the Views of Global Warming Deniers

Brendan O'Neill

Brendan O'Neill argues in the following viewpoint that many in the media and in the public at large are rejecting the views of global warming deniers without reasoned debate. This intolerance, O'Neill claims, is the result of an organized environmentalist plan to silence the opinions of naysayers and give the impression that there is only one correct view concerning global climate change. In O'Neill's opinion, regardless of whose argument is proven accurate, the trend toward environmentalist authoritarianism should be a worry to all who value free speech and open debate. Brendan O'Neill is a London-based journalist and the editor of Spiked Online, *an Internet news magazine.*

Brendan O'Neill, "Global Warming: The Chilling Effect on Free Speech," *Spiked Online*, October 6, 2006. Reproduced by permission.

As you read, consider the following questions:

1. Why does O'Neill find it shameful that England's Royal Society would try to compel ExxonMobil to stop funding organizations that deny the theory of global warming?

2. According to O'Neill, what was the response of the current affairs television show *60 Minutes* when it was asked why its program on global warming did not include the views of skeptics?

3. For what two reasons does the author find it "deeply repugnant" to draw correlations between the Holocaust and climate change debate?

The message is clear: climate change deniers are scum. Their words are so wicked and dangerous that they must be silenced, or criminalised, or forced beyond the pale alongside those other crackpots who claim there was no Nazi Holocaust against the Jews. Perhaps climate change deniers should even be killed off, hanged like those evil men who were tried Nuremberg-style the first time around.

Whatever the truth about our warming planet, it is clear there is a tidal wave of intolerance in the debate about climate change which is eroding free speech and melting rational debate. There has been no decree from on high or piece of legislation outlawing climate change denial, and indeed there is no need to criminalise it. ... Because in recent months it has been turned into a taboo, chased out of polite society by a wink and a nod, letters of complaint, newspaper articles continually comparing climate change denial to Holocaust denial. An attitude of 'You can't say that!' now surrounds debates about climate change, which in many ways is more powerful and pernicious than an outright ban. I am not a scientist or an expert on climate change, but I know what I don't like—

and this demonisation of certain words and ideas is an affront to freedom of speech and open, rational debate.

A Pejorative Term

The loaded term itself—"climate change denier"—is used to mark out certain people as immoral, untrustworthy. According to Richard D North, author most recently of *Rich is Beautiful: A Very Personal Defence of Mass Affluence:* "It is deeply pejorative to call someone a "climate change denier" . . . it is a phrase designedly reminiscent of the idea of Holocaust denial—the label applied to those misguided or wicked people who believe, or claim to believe, the Nazis did not annihilate the Jews, and others, in very great numbers." People of various views and hues tend to get lumped together under the umbrella put-down "climate change denier"—from those who argue the planet is getting hotter but we will be able to deal with it, to those who claim the planet is unlikely to get much hotter at all. On Google there are now over 80,000 search returns, and counting, for the phrase climate change denial.

Others take the tactic of openly labelling climate change deniers as cranks, possibly even people who might need their heads checked. In a speech last month [September 2006], in which he said people "should be scared" about global warming, UK environment secretary David Miliband said "those who deny [climate change] are the flat-earthers of the twenty-first century". Taking a similar tack, former US vice president-turned-green-warrior Al Gore recently declared: "Fifteen per cent of the population believe the moon landing was actually staged in a movie lot in Arizona and somewhat fewer still believe the Earth is flat. I think they all get together with the global warming deniers on a Saturday night and party."

Scientific Strong-Arming

It is not only environmentalist activists and green-leaning writers who are seeking to silence climate change deniers/

sceptics/critics/whatever you prefer. [In September] the Royal Society—Britain's premier scientific academy founded in 1660, whose members have included some of the greatest scientists—wrote a letter to ExxonMobil demanding that the oil giant cut off its funding to groups that have "misrepresented the science of climate change by outright denial of the evidence". It was the first time the Royal Society had ever written to a company complaining about its activities. The letter had something of a hectoring, intolerant tone: "At our meeting in July [2006] . . . you indicated that ExxonMobil would not be providing any further funding to these organisations. I would be grateful if you could let me know when ExxonMobil plans to carry out this pledge."

One could be forgiven for asking what business it is of the Royal Society to tell ExxonMobil whom it can and cannot support—just as we might balk if ExxonMobil tried to tell the Royal Society what to do. The Society claims it is merely defending a "scientific consensus . . . the evidence" against ExxonMobil's duplicitous attempts to play down global warming for its own oily self-interest. Yet some scientists have attacked the idea that there can ever be untouchable cast-iron scientific facts, which should be immune from debate or protected from oil-moneyed think-tanks. An open letter to the Society—signed by Tim Ball, a professor of climatology at the University of Winnipeg, and others—argues that "scientific inquiry is unique because it requires falsifiability": "The beauty of science is that no issue is ever 'settled', that no question is beyond being more fully understood, that no conclusion is immune to further experimentation. And yet for the first time in history, the Royal Society is shamelessly using the media to say emphatically: 'case closed' on all issues related to climate change."

Or as Charles Jones, an emeritus English professor at the University of Edinburgh, put it in a letter to a publication that recently lambasted climate change deniers, "[W]e are left with the feeling that [climate change] is a scientific model which is unfalsifiable and which has not been—and indeed cannot be—the subject of any theoretical counter-proposals whatsoever. As such, it must surely be unique in the history of science. Even a powerful model such as Relativity Theory has been the object of scientific debate and emendation."

From Skeptics to Heretics

For all the talk of simply preserving the facts against climate change deniers, there is increasingly a pernicious moralism and authoritarianism in the attempts to silence certain individuals and groups. This is clear from the use of the term "climate change denier", which, as Charles Jones argued, is an attempt to assign any "doubters" with "the same moral repugnance one associates with Holocaust denial". The *Guardian* columnist George Monbiot recently celebrated the 'recanting' of both the tabloid *Sun* and the business bible *The Economist* on the issue of global warming. ("Recant"—an interesting choice of word. According to my *OED* [*Oxford English Dictionary*] it means "To withdraw, retract or renounce a statement, opinion or belief as erroneous, and *esp.* with formal or public confession of error in matters of religion." Recanting is often what those accused before the Spanish Inquisition did to save their hides.) Pleased by the *Sun* and *The Economist*'s turnaround, Monbiot wrote: "Almost everywhere, climate change denial now looks as stupid and as unacceptable as Holocaust denial."

Earlier [in 2006], when a correspondent for the American current affairs show *60 Minutes* was asked why his various feature programmes on global warming did not include the views of global warming sceptics, he replied: "If I do an interview with Elie Wiesel, am I required as a journalist to find a Holocaust denier?" Here, climate change deniers are explicitly painted as the bad guys. He also argued that, "This isn't about politics . . . this is about sound science", and went so far as to

News Networks Shut out Dissent

To better assess network behavior on [global warming], the Business & Media Institute [BMI] examined 205 stories from ABC, CBS and NBC that mentioned "global warming" or "climate change" between July 1, 2007, and Dec. 31, 2007.

BMI found skepticism was shut out of a vast majority of reports. Overall, a measly 20 percent had any dissent at all referenced by a journalist or guest.

Skeptical voices were suppressed by the networks, outnumbered by nearly a 7-to-1 ratio by those promoting fear of climate change or being used by the network for the same purpose. CBS had an even worse record: nearly 38 proponents to one skeptic.

Julia A. Seymour and Dan Gainor,
Global Warming Censored: How the Major Networks
Silence the Debate on Global Warming
Global Research, April 9, 2008. www.globalresearch.ca

claim that it would be problematic even to air the views of climate change sceptics: "There comes a point in journalism where striving for balance becomes irresponsible."

Some take the moral equivalence between climate change denial and Holocaust denial to its logical conclusion. They argue that climate change deniers are actually complicit in a future Holocaust—the global warming Holocaust—and thus will have to be brought to trial in the future. Green author and columnist Mark Lynas writes: "I wonder what sentences judges might hand down at future international criminal tribunals on those who will be partially but directly responsible for millions of deaths from starvation, famine and disease in decades ahead. I put [their climate change denial] in a similar moral category to Holocaust denial—except that this time the Holocaust is yet to come, and we still have time to avoid it. Those who try to ensure we don't will one day have to answer for their crimes."

Comparing Proven History with Unproven Future Predictions

There is something deeply repugnant in marshalling the Holocaust in this way, both to berate climate change deniers and also as a convenient snapshot of what is to come if the planet continues to get warmer. First, the evidence is irrefutable that six million Jews were murdered by the Nazis; that is an historical event that has been thoroughly investigated, interrogated and proven beyond reasonable doubt. (Although as the American-Jewish academic and warrior against Holocaust denial, Deborah Lipstadt, has pointed out, even the Nazi Holocaust is not above debate and re-evaluation; it is not a "theology".) There is no such proof or evidence (how could there be?) that global warming will cause a similar calamity. Second, it is, yet again, a cynical attempt to close down debate. The H-word is uttered as a kind of moral absolute that no one could possibly question. We are all against what happened during the first Holocaust, so we will be against the "next Holocaust", too, right? And if not—if you do not take seriously the coming "global warming Holocaust"—then you are clearly wicked, the equivalent of the David Irvings of this world, someone who should possibly even be locked up or certainly tried at a future date. At least laws against Holocaust denial (which, as a supporter of free speech, I am opposed to) chastise individuals for lying about a known and proven event; by contrast, the turning of climate change denial into a taboo raps people on the knuckles for questioning events, or alleged events, that have not even occurred yet. It is pre-emptive censorship. They are reprimanded not for lying, but for doubting, for questioning. If this approach was taken across the board, then [online news site] *spiked*—motto: Question Everything—would be in for a rough ride.

Sometimes there is a knowing authoritarianism in green activism. The posters advertising George Monbiot's new book are targeted at various celebrities and businessmen judged to be living less than ethical green lives, with the words "George Is Watching You". It comes straight out of [British writer George] Orwell's *Nineteen Eighty-Four*. Some institutions employ Orwellian doublespeak when they use the word "facts". They are not talking about submitting theories or hypotheses or evidence for public debate and possibly public approval—they are talking about using "facts" precisely to stifle public debate and change the way people think and behave.

No Interest in Debate

So in a report on global warming titled *Warm Words: How Are We Telling the Climate Story and Can We Tell it Better?*, the British think-tank the Institute for Public Policy Research [IPPR] argued that "the task of climate change agencies is not to persuade by rational argument but in effect to develop and nurture a new 'common sense'. . . . [We] need to work in a more shrewd and contemporary way, using subtle techniques of engagement. . . . The 'facts' need to be treated as being so taken-for-granted that they need not be spoken." The IPPR proposes treating us not as free-thinking citizens who should be engaged, but as consumers who should be sold these "unspoken facts": "Ultimately, positive climate behaviours need to be approached in the same way as marketeers approach acts of buying and consuming. . . . It amounts to treating climate-friendly activity as a brand that can be sold. This is, we believe, the route to mass behaviour changes."

Nurturing a new common sense? Changing mass behaviour? Behind the talk of facts and figures we can glimpse the reality: an authoritarian campaign that has no interest whatsoever in engaging us in debate but rather thinks up "shrewd" ways to change the way we behave. From the description of facts as "so taken-for-granted that they need not be spoken" to the lumping together of climate change deniers with Holocaust deniers—and even Holocaust practitioners—we can see a creeping clampdown on any genuine, open debate about climate change, science and society. This represents a dangerous denigration of free speech. When George W. Bush said after 9/11 "You're either with us or against us", he was widely criticised. Yet greens, think-tanks, reputable institutions and government ministers are using precisely the same tactic, drawing a line between good and proper people who accept the facts about climate change and those moral lepers who do not; between those who submit to having their common sense nurtured by the powers-that-be and those who dare to doubt or debate.

If anything, the greens' black-and-white divide is worse than Bush's. At least his was based on some kind of values, allowing us the opportunity to say yes or no to them; the greens' divide is based on "facts"; which means that those who decide that they are "against" rather than "with" can be labelled liars, deniers or crackpots like moon-landing conspiracy theorists or anti-Semitic historians.

Environmental Authoritarianism Should Be a Concern

Effectively, campaigners and officials are using scientific facts—over which there is still disagreement—to shut down what ought to be a *political* debate about what humans need and want. This is the worst of it. Whatever side you take in the climate change clash of facts, this undermining of debate should be a cause of concern. In place of a human-centred discussion of priorities and solutions we have an unconvincing battle over the facts between two sides—between those in the majority who claim that their facts show the planet is getting a lot hotter and it will be a disaster, and those in the minority, the "deniers", who say the planet is getting a little hotter and it won't be so bad. We could urgently do with a proper debate that prioritises real people's aspirations. If parts of the planet are likely to be flooded, then where can we build new cities and how can we transport the people affected by the floods to those cities? If natural disasters are going to become more frequent, then how can we urgently and efficiently provide poorer parts of the world with the kind of buildings and technology that will allow them to ride out such disasters, as millions do in America every year?

We need to elevate the human interest over the dead discussion of fatalistic facts—and challenge the "You can't say that!" approach that is strangling debate and giving rise to a new authoritarianism.

| "The doubters aren't interested in things like data and observations and peer-reviewed research."

Science Disproves the Claims of Global Warming Deniers

Joseph Romm

Joseph Romm is an author and scientist. He is a Senior Fellow at the Center for American Progress, a liberal public policy institute, where he writes chiefly about global warming and greenhouse gases. In the following viewpoint, Romm contends that the views of climate change deniers are scientifically inaccurate. As Romm states, scientific facts show that global warming is occurring and that humans are responsible for the changing climate. He refutes conjectures that natural forces are to blame and chastises skeptics for attempting to persuade the public that fears about global warming are not based on verifiable evidence.

As you read, consider the following questions:

1. How does Romm show that science does not work by consensus of opinion?

Joseph Romm, "The Cold Truth About Climate Change," *Salon.com*, February 27, 2008. This article first appeared in Salon.com, at http://www.salon.com. An online version remains in the Salon archives. Reprinted with permission.

2. How does Romm explain away the theory that the sun is the primary force behind global warming?

3. As Romm reports, how are IPCC reports "lowballing" predictions about the future impact of global warming?

The more I write about global warming, the more I realize I share some things in common with the doubters and deniers who populate the blogosphere and the conservative movement. Like them, I am dubious about the process used by the U.N. Intergovernmental Panel on Climate Change (IPCC) to write its reports. Like them, I am skeptical of the so-called consensus on climate science as reflected in the IPCC reports. Like them, I disagree with people who say "the science is settled." But that's where the agreement ends.

The science isn't settled—it's unsettling, and getting more so every year as the scientific community learns more about the catastrophic consequences of uncontrolled greenhouse gas emissions.

Humans Are at Fault

The big difference I have with the doubters is they believe the IPCC reports seriously overstate the impact of human emissions on the climate, whereas the actual observed climate data clearly show the reports dramatically understate the impact.

But I do think the scientific community, the progressive community, environmentalists and media are making a serious mistake by using the word "consensus" to describe the shared understanding scientists have about the ever-worsening impacts that human-caused greenhouse gas emissions are having on this planet. When scientists and others say there is a consensus, many if not most people probably hear "consensus of opinion," which can—and often is—dismissed out of hand. I've met lots of people like CNBC anchor Joe Kernen, who simply can't believe that "as old as the planet is" that "puny, gnawing little humans" could possibly change the climate in "70 years."

Well, Joe, it is more like 250 years, but yes, most of the damage to date was done in the last 70 years, and yes, as counterintuitive as it may seem, puny little humans are doing it, and it's going to get much, much worse unless we act soon. Consensus of opinion is irrelevant to science because reality is often counterintuitive—just try studying quantum mechanics.

Fortunately Kernen wasn't around when scientists were warning that puny little humans were destroying the Earth's protective ozone layer. Otherwise we might never have banned chlorofluorocarbons in time.

Consensus of opinion is also dismissed as groupthink. In a December [2007] article ignorantly titled "The Science of Gore's Nobel: What If Everyone Believes in Global Warmism Only Because Everyone Believes in Global Warmism?" Holman W. Jenkins Jr. of the *Wall Street Journal* [WSJ] editorial board wrote:

> What if the heads being counted to certify an alleged "consensus" arrived at their positions by counting heads?
>
> It may seem strange that scientists would participate in such a phenomenon. It shouldn't. Scientists are human; they do not wait for proof. Many devote their professional lives to seeking evidence for hypotheses, especially well-funded hypotheses, they've chosen to believe.
>
> Less surprising is the readiness of many prominent journalists to embrace the role of enforcer of an orthodoxy simply because it is the orthodoxy. For them, a consensus apparently suffices as proof of itself.

How sad that the WSJ and CNBC have so little conception of what science really is, especially since scientific advances drive so much of the economy. If that's what Jenkins thinks science is, one would assume he is equally skeptical of flossing, antibiotics and even boarding an airplane.

(Note to WSJ: One reason science works is that a lot of scientists devote their whole lives to overturning whatever is the current hypothesis—if it can be overturned. That's how you become famous and remembered by history, like Copernicus, Galileo, Newton, Darwin and Einstein.)

Science Has Nothing to Do with Consensus

In fact, science doesn't work by consensus of opinion. Science is in many respects the exact opposite of decision by consensus. General opinion at one point might have been that the sun goes around the Earth, or that time was an absolute quantity, but scientific theory supported by observations overturned that flawed worldview.

One of the most serious results of the overuse of the term "consensus" in the public discussion of global warming is that it creates a simple strategy for doubters to confuse the public, the press and politicians: Simply come up with as long a list as you can of scientists who dispute the theory. After all, such disagreement is prima facie proof that no consensus of opinion exists.

So we end up with the absurd but pointless spectacle of the leading denier in the U.S. Senate, James Inhofe, R-Okla., who [in December 2007] put out a list of more than 400 names of supposedly "prominent scientists" who supposedly "recently voiced significant objections to major aspects of the so-called 'consensus' on man-made global warming."

As it turned out, the list is both padded and laughable, containing the opinions of TV weathermen, economists, a bunch of non-prominent scientists who aren't climate experts, and, perhaps surprisingly, even a number of people who actually believe in the consensus.

But in any case, nothing could be more irrelevant to climate science than the opinion of people on the list such as

Weather Channel founder John Coleman or famed inventor Ray Kurzweil (who actually does "think global warming is real"). Or, for that matter, my opinion—even though I researched a Ph.D. thesis at the Scripps Institution of Oceanography on physical oceanography in the Greenland Sea.

Science Has Everything to Do with Fact

What matters is scientific findings—data, not opinions. The IPCC relies on the peer-reviewed scientific literature for its conclusions, which must meet the rigorous requirements of the scientific method and which are inevitably scrutinized by others seeking to disprove that work. That is why I cite and link to as much research as is possible, hundreds of studies in the case of this article. Opinions are irrelevant.

A good example of how scientific evidence drives our understanding concerns how we know that humans are the dominant cause of global warming. This is, of course, the deniers' favorite topic. Since it is increasingly obvious that the climate is changing and the planet is warming, the remaining deniers have coalesced to defend their Alamo—that human emissions aren't the cause of recent climate change and therefore that reducing those emissions is pointless.

[In 2007], longtime *Nation* columnist Alexander Cockburn wrote, "There is still zero empirical evidence that anthropogenic production of CO_2 is making any measurable contribution to the world's present warming trend. The greenhouse fearmongers rely entirely on unverified, crudely oversimplified computer models to finger mankind's sinful contribution."

In fact, the evidence is amazingly strong. Moreover, if the relatively complex climate models are oversimplified in any respect, it is by omitting amplifying feedbacks and other factors that suggest human-caused climate change will be worse than is widely realized.

The IPCC concluded [in 2007]: "Greenhouse gas forcing has very likely (>90 percent) caused most of the observed global warming over the last 50 years. This conclusion takes into account ... the possibility that the response to solar forcing could be underestimated by climate models."

Scientists have come to understand that "forcings" (natural and human-made) explain most of the changes in our climate and temperature both in recent decades and over the past millions of years. The primary human-made forcings are the heat-trapping greenhouse gases we generate, particularly carbon dioxide from burning coal, oil and natural gas. The natural forcings include fluctuations in the intensity of sunlight (which can increase or decrease warming), and major volcanoes that inject huge volumes of gases and aerosol particles into the stratosphere (which tend to block sunlight and cause cooling).

A 2002 study by the U.S. National Academy of Sciences warned, "Abrupt climate changes were especially common when the climate system was being forced to change most rapidly." The rapidly growing greenhouse warming we ourselves are causing today thus increases the chances for "large, abrupt and unwelcome regional or global climatic events."

Global Warming Is Not Caused by Natural Forcings Alone

Over and over again, scientists have demonstrated that observed changes in the climate in recent decades can only be explained by taking into account the observed combination of human and natural forcings. Natural forcings alone just don't explain what is happening to this planet.

For instance, in April 2005, one of the nation's top climate scientists, NASA's James Hansen, led a team of scientists that made "precise measurements of increasing ocean heat content over the past 10 years," which revealed that the Earth is absorbing far more heat than it is emitting to space, confirming what earlier computer models had shown about warming, Hansen called this energy imbalance the "smoking gun" of climate change, and said, "There can no longer be genuine doubt that human-made gases are the dominant cause of observed warming."

Another 2005 study, led by the Scripps Institution of Oceanography, compared actual ocean temperature data from the surface down to hundreds of meters (in the Atlantic, Pacific and Indian oceans) with climate models and concluded:

> A warming signal has penetrated into the world's oceans over the past 40 years. The signal is complex, with a vertical structure that varies widely by ocean; it cannot be explained by natural internal climate variability or solar and volcanic forcing, but is well simulated by two anthropogenically [human-caused] forced climate models. We conclude that it is of human origin, a conclusion robust to observational sampling and model differences.

Such studies are also done for many other observations: land-based temperature rise, atmospheric temperature rise, sea level rise, arctic ice melt, inland glacier melt, Greenland and Antarctic ice sheet melt, expansion of the tropics (desertification) and changes in precipitation. Studies compare every testable prediction from climate change theory and models (and suggested by paleoclimate research) to actual observations.

How many studies? Well, the IPCC's definitive treatment of the subject, "Understanding and Attributing Climate Change," has 11 full pages of references, some 500 peer-reviewed studies. This is not a consensus of opinion. It is what scientific research and actual observations reveal.

Problems with a Solar Explanation

Ignoring all the evidence, doubters and deniers keep asserting that the cause of global warming isn't human emissions, but is instead natural forcings, primarily the sun. [In 2007], brief

The Lingering Impact of Denial

Since the late 1980s, [a] well-coordinated, well-funded campaign by contrarian scientists, free-market think tanks and industry has created a paralyzing fog of doubt around climate change. Through advertisements, op-eds, lobbying and media attention, greenhouse doubters (they hate being called deniers) argued first that the world is not warming; measurements indicating otherwise are flawed, they said. Then they claimed that any warming is natural, not caused by human activities. Now they contend that the looming warming will be minuscule and harmless. . . .

[In 2006], polls found that 64 percent of Americans thought there was "a lot" of scientific disagreement on climate change; only one third thought planetary warming was "mainly caused by things people do." In contrast, majorities in Europe and Japan recognize a broad consensus among climate experts that greenhouse gases— mostly from the burning of coal, oil and natural gas to power the world's economies—are altering climate. A [2007] *Newsweek* Poll finds that the influence of the denial machine remains strong. Although the figure is less than in earlier polls, 39 percent of those asked say there is "a lot of disagreement among climate scientists" on the basic question of whether the planet is warming. . . . Only 46 percent say the greenhouse effect is being felt today.

Sharon Begley,
Newsweek, *August 13, 2007.*

presidential candidate Fred Thompson commented on claims that planets like Mars were supposedly also warming—an idea debunked by RealClimate. Thompson said sarcastically:

I wonder what all those planets, dwarf planets and moons in our *solar* system have in common. Hmmmm. *Solar* system. Hmmmm. Solar? I wonder. Nah, I guess we shouldn't even be talking about this. The science is absolutely decided. There's a consensus. Ask Galileo.

The view that the sun is the source of observed global warming seems credible mainly to people who are open to believing that the entire scientific community has somehow, over a period of several decades, failed to adequately study, analyze and understand the most visible influence on the Earth's temperature. Such people typically cannot be influenced by the results of actual research and observations. Those who can should visit Skeptical Science, which discusses deniers' favorite arguments. In one discussion, the site explains that the "study most quoted by skeptics actually concluded the sun can't be causing global warming." Doh!

And that brings us to a [2007] study by the Proceedings of the Royal Society, which examined "all the trends in the Sun that could have had an influence on the Earth's climate," such as sunlight intensity and cosmic rays. The study found that in the past 20 years, all of those trends "have been in the opposite direction to that required to explain the observed rise in global mean temperatures."

Those trying to prove the sun is the sole cause of warming have a double challenge. First they would have to show us a mechanism that demonstrates how the sun explains recent warming, even though the data shows solar activity has been declining recently. (In the past, increased warming was associated with an increase in solar activity.) They would also have to find an additional mechanism that is counteracting the well-understood warming caused by rising emissions of heat-trapping greenhouse gases. The doubters have done neither.

The Rise in Carbon Dioxide

But then the doubters aren't interested in things like data and observations and peer-reviewed research. If they were, why would they keep pointing out that, historically, global temperature rise precedes a rise in carbon dioxide emissions by a few hundred years—as if that were a reason to cast doubt on the impact of human emissions of greenhouse gases? Rep. Joe Barton said to Al Gore:

> I have an article from *Science* magazine that explains a rise in CO_2 concentrations actually lagged temperature by 200 to 1000 years. CO_2 levels went up after the temperature rose. Temperature appears to drive CO_2, not vice versa. You're not just off a little. You're totally wrong.

Yes, historically, glacial periods appear to end with an initial warming started by changes in the Earth's orbit around the sun. This in turn leads to increases in carbon dioxide (and methane), which then accelerate the warming, which increases the emissions, which increases the warming. That amplifying feedback in the global carbon cycle is what drives the global temperature to change so fast.

But while this fact seems to make doubters less worried about the impact of human emissions, it makes most scientists more worried. As famed climatologist Wallace Broecker wrote in *Nature* in 1995:

> The paleoclimate record shouts out to us that, far from being self-stabilizing, the Earth's climate system is an ornery beast which overreacts even to small nudges.

That is, you need a trigger to start the process of rapid climate change. Historically, that has been orbital changes, or sometimes, massive natural releases of greenhouse gases.

Now humans have interrupted and overwhelmed the natural process of climate change. Thanks to humans, carbon dioxide levels are higher than they have been for millions of years. Even more worrisome, carbon dioxide emissions are rising 200 times faster than at any time in the last 650,000 years.

If the "Earth's climate system is an ornery beast which overreacts even to small nudges," what will happen to people foolish enough to keep punching it in the face?

IPCC Models and Political Wrangling

That brings us to another problem with the word "consensus." It can mean "unanimity" or "the judgment arrived at by most of those concerned." Many, if not most, people hear the second meaning: "consensus" as majority opinion.

The scientific consensus most people are familiar with is the IPCC's "Summary for Policymakers" reports. But those aren't a majority opinion. Government representatives participate in a line-by-line review and revision of these summaries. So China, Saudi Arabia and that hotbed of denialism—the [George W.] Bush administration—get to veto anything they don't like. The deniers call this "politicized science," suggesting the process turns the IPCC summaries into some sort of unscientific exaggeration. In fact, the reverse is true. The net result is unanimous agreement on a conservative or watered-down document. You could argue that rather than majority rules, this is "minority rules."

[In] April [2007], in an article titled "Conservative Climate," *Scientific American* noted that objections by Saudi Arabia and China led the IPCC to remove a sentence stating that the impact of human greenhouse gas emissions on the Earth's recent warming is five times greater than that of the sun. In fact, lead author Piers Forster of the University of Leeds in England said, "The difference is really a factor of 10."

How decent of the IPCC not to smash the last hope of deniers like Fred Thompson, whose irrational sun worshiping allows them to ignore the overwhelming evidence that human emissions are the dominant cause of climate change.

How else does the IPCC lowball future impacts? The 2007 report projects sea level rise this century of 7 to 23 inches. Yet the IPCC itself stated that "models [of sea level rise] used to date do not include uncertainties in climate-carbon cycle feedbacks nor do they include the full effect of changes in ice sheet flow."

That is, since no existing climate models fully account for the kinds of feedbacks we are now witnessing in Greenland and Antarctica, such as dynamic acceleration of ice sheet disintegration or greenhouse gases released by melting tundra, the IPCC is forced to ignore those realities. The result is that compared to the "consensus" of the IPCC, the ice sheets appear to be shrinking "100 years ahead of schedule," as Penn State climatologist Richard Alley put it in March 2006.

According to both the 2001 and 2007 IPCC reports, neither Greenland nor Antarctica should lose significant mass by 2100. They both already are. Here again, the conservative nature of the IPCC process puts it at odds with observed empirical realities that are the basis of all science.

It's no surprise then that three scientific studies released in [2007]—too late for inclusion by the IPCC—argue that based on historical data and recent observations, sea level rise this century will be much higher than the IPCC reports, up to 5 feet or more. Even scarier, the rate of sea level rise in 2100 might be greater than 6 inches a decade!

And it's no surprise at all that sea-level rise from 1993 and 2006—1.3 inches per decade as measured by satellites—has been higher than the IPCC climate models predicted.

The deniers are simply wrong when they claim that the IPCC has overestimated either current or future warming impacts. As many other recent observations reveal, the IPCC has been underestimating those impacts.

- Since 2000, carbon dioxide emissions have grown faster than any IPCC model had projected.

- The temperature rise from 1990 to 2005—0.33°C—was "near the top end of the range" of IPCC climate model predictions.

- "The recent [Arctic] sea-ice retreat is larger than in any of the (19) IPCC [climate] models"—and that was a

Norwegian expert in 2005. Since then, the Arctic retreat has stunned scientists by accelerating, losing an area equal to Texas and California just last summer.

- "The unexpectedly rapid expansion of the tropical belt constitutes yet another signal that climate change is occurring sooner than expected," noted one climate researcher in December [2007].

More Recent and Dire Predictions

This last point, though little remarked on in the media, should be as worrisome as the unexpectedly rapid melting of the ice sheets. As a [2007] study led by NOAA [National Oceanic and Atmospheric Administration] noted, "A poleward expansion of the tropics is likely to bring even drier conditions to" the U.S. Southwest, Mexico, Australia and parts of Africa and South America. Also: "An increase in the width of the tropics could bring an increase in the area affected by tropical storms." And finally: "An expansion of tropical pathogens and their insect vectors is almost certainly sure to follow the expansion of tropical zones."

Why are recent observations on the high side of model projections? First, as noted, most climate models used by the IPCC omit key amplifying feedbacks in the carbon cycle. Second, it was widely thought that increased human carbon dioxide emissions would be partly offset by more trees and other vegetation. But increases in droughts and wildfires—both predicted by global warming theory—seem to have negated that. Third, the ocean—one of the largest sinks for carbon dioxide—seems to be saturating decades earlier than the models had projected.

The result, as a number of studies have shown, is that the sensitivity of the world's climate to human emissions of greenhouse gases is no doubt much higher than the sensitivity used in most IPCC models. NASA's Hansen argued in a paper [in 2007] that the climate ultimately has twice the sensitivity used in IPCC models.

The bottom line is that recent observations and research make clear the planet almost certainly faces a greater and more imminent threat than is laid out in the IPCC reports. That's why climate scientists are so desperate. That's why they keep begging for immediate action. And that's why the "consensus on global warming" is a phrase that should be forever retired from the climate debate.

| "As serious scientists repeatedly explain, global cooling is here."

The Earth's Climate Is Cooling, Not Warming

Deroy Murdock

In the viewpoint that follows, Deroy Murdock points out that many normally warm climates have experienced cooler temperatures—even snowfall—in recent years. Some scientists refer to this trend as global cooling, and Murdock, citing several of these experts, suggests that global warming alarmism may be unfounded. Deroy Murdock is a columnist with Scripps Howard News Service and a media fellow with the Hoover Institution on War, Revolution and Peace at Stanford University.

As you read, consider the following questions:

1. On December 17, 2008, how much snow fell on the hills of Malibu, California, as Murdock reports?

2. As Murdock suggests, what phenomenon may underlie the dropping temperatures in 2008?

3. What two climate variables does Murdock say the IPCC ignored when it made its prediction of a forthcoming global temperature rise?

Deroy Murdock, "Global Cooling?" *The Washington Times*, December 21, 2008. Reproduced by permission.

Winter officially arrives today [December 21] with the solstice. But for many Americans, autumn 2008's final days already felt like deepest, coldest January.

Some New Englanders still lack electricity after a Dec. 11 ice storm snapped power lines. Up to eight inches of snow struck New Orleans and southern Louisiana that day and didn't melt for 48 hours in some neighborhoods.

In southern California Dec. 17, a half-inch of snow brightened Malibu's hills while a half-foot barricaded highways and marooned commuters in desert towns east of Los Angeles. Three inches of the white stuff shuttered Las Vegas' McCarren Airport that day and dusted the Strip's hotels and casinos.

What are the odds of that?

Actually, the odds are rising that snow, ice and cold will grow increasingly common. As serious scientists repeatedly explain, global cooling is here. It is chilling temperatures and so-called "global-warming."

According to the National Climatic Data Center, 2008 will be America's coldest year since 1997, thanks to La Niña and precipitation in the central and eastern states. Solar quietude also may underlie global cooling. This year's sunspots and solar radiation approach the minimum in the sun's cycle, corresponding with lower Earth temperatures. This echoes Harvard-Smithsonian astrophysicist Dr. Sallie Baliunas' belief that solar variability, much more than CO_2, sways global temperatures.

Meanwhile, the National Weather Service reports that last summer was Anchorage's third coldest on record. "Not since 1980 has there been a summer less reflective of global warming," Craig Medred wrote in the Anchorage Daily News. Consequently, Alaska's glaciers are thickening in the middle. "It's been a long time on most glaciers where they've actually had positive mass balance," U.S. Geological Survey glaciologist Bruce Molnia told Mr. Medred Oct. 13. Similarly, the National Snow and Ice Data Center found that Arctic sea ice expanded 13.2 percent this year, or a Texas-sized 270,000 square miles.

Global warming or not, it's still freezing here...

"Global warming or not, it's still freezing in here, . . ." cartoon by Hagen.
WWWCartoonStock.com.

Across the equator, Brazil endured an especially cold September. Snow graced its southern provinces that month.

"Global Warming is over, and Global Warming Theory has failed. There is no evidence that CO_2 drives world temperatures or any consequent climate change," Imperial College London astrophysicist and long-range forecaster Piers Corbyn wrote British members of Parliament on Oct. 28. "According to official data in every year since 1998, world temperatures have been colder than that year, yet CO_2 has been rising rapidly." That evening, as the House of Commons debated legislation on so-called "global warming," October snow fell in London for the first time since 1922.

These observations parallel those of five German researchers led by Professor Noel Keenlyside of the Leibniz Institute of Marine Sciences. "Our results suggest that global surface temperature may not increase over the next decade," they concluded in last May's *Nature*, "as natural climate variations in the North Atlantic and tropical Pacific temporarily offset the projected anthropogenic (man-made) warming."

This "lull" should doom the 0.54 degree Fahrenheit average global temperature rise predicted by the U.N.'s Intergovernmental Panel on Climate Change [IPCC], the Vatican of so-called "global warming." Incidentally, the IPCC's computer models factor in neither El Niño nor the Gulf Stream. Excluding such major climate variables would be like ESPN [Entertainment and Sports Programming Network] ignoring baseball and basketball.

So, is this all just propaganda concocted by Chevron-funded, right-wing, flat-Earthers? Ask Dr. Martin Hertzberg, a physical chemist and retired Navy meteorologist.

"As a scientist and life-long liberal Democrat, I find the constant regurgitation of the anecdotal, fear-mongering claptrap about human-caused global warming to be a disservice to science," Mr. Hertzberg wrote in Sept. 26's *USA Today*. "From the El Niño year of 1998 until Jan., 2007, the average temperature of the Earth's atmosphere near its surface decreased some 0.25°C (0.45°F). From Jan., 2007 until the spring of 2008, it dropped a whopping 0.75°C (1.35°F)."

As global cooling becomes more widely recognized, Americans from Maine to Malibu should feel comfortable dreaming of a white Christmas.

Periodical Bibliography

The following articles have been selected to supplement the diverse views presented in this chapter.

Lawrence Downes	"A Disappointing Truth," *The New York Times*, July 20, 2008.
Dan Fitzpatrick and Robert Lee Hotz	"Scientists Remain Divided Over Issue of Changing Patterns in Storms," *Wall Street Journal*, September 2, 2008.
Human Events	"Top Ten 'Global-Warming' Myths," February 19, 2007.
William Kininmoth	"Illusions of Climate Science," *Quadrant* magazine, October 2008.
Joseph Romm	"End This Addiction Immediately," *U.S. News & World Report*, July 21, 2008.
Matthew Rothschild	"Global Warming Challenge," *Progressive*, September 2008.
Walter Starck	"Global Warming—Myth, Threat or Opportunity?" *National Observer*, Summer 2008.
Moises Velasquez-Manoff	"How to Spur Action on Global Warming," *Christian Science Monitor*, November 5, 2008.
The Washington Times	"Global-Warming Myth," May 16, 2008.

OPPOSING
VIEWPOINTS®
SERIES

CHAPTER 2

What Causes Global Warming?

Chapter Preface

Henrik Svensmark, the director of the Center for Sun-Climate Research at the Danish National Space Center, is one of several scientists who claim that the impact of human-made pollution on global warming may not be as strong as commonly believed. In Svensmark's estimation, solar activity is a prime culprit of global warming and even global cooling. As Svensmark told *Discover* magazine in 2007, cosmic rays from distant supernovas are responsible for cloud formations on earth. These rays must pass through the magnetic field of the sun before reaching the planets, and if there is a great amount of solar wind and other activity, fewer rays will penetrate. "Fewer cosmic rays mean fewer clouds will be formed, and so there will be a warmer Earth. If the sun and the solar wind are not so active, then more cosmic rays can come in. That means more clouds [reflecting away more sunlight] and a cooler Earth," Svensmark attests. He maintains that the Little Ice Age that began in the 1600s is evidence of a period in which the earth cooled because of decreased solar activity, and conversely now that the sun is more active, the planet is heating up.

Habibullo Abdussamatov, the head of space research at St. Petersburg's Pulkovo Astronomical Observatory in Russia, agrees with Svensmark's findings and even claims that human-made carbon emissions are not nearly as significant a factor in global warming as solar activity. "Man-made greenhouse warming has made a small contribution to the warming seen on Earth in recent years, but it cannot compete with the increase in solar irradiance," Abdussamatov told National Geographic News in 2007. Using his calculations of solar trends, the Russian scientist is convinced that earth is heading for a sharp—perhaps disastrous—cooling in the next two decades.

Both Svensmark and Abdussamatov have received a good deal of criticism for their views. The majority of climatologists agree that carbon dioxide and other greenhouse gases are the drivers of climate change. Although natural forces may have some impact in the theories expounded by this majority, these scientists contend that natural and human-produced emissions of carbon dioxide, methane, and nitrous oxide have a more profound effect on the climate. A 2007 study from Britain argues that solar activity has little or no effect on global temperatures. Examining records of sunspots and other solar events, this team of scientists could find no correlation between current solar activity and rising temperatures. "Nobody can show that there is no solar/Earth climate connection," Carl Wunsch, a Massachusetts Institute of Technology climate expert noted after having looked at the British report. "But having said that, if there is one and if these records are representative, whatever connection exists is weak."

In the following chapter, various climate researchers give their opinions on what factors are contributing to global warming and how important these factors are in any predicted climate change.

"Climate scientists attribute the pre-industrial level of CO_2 to natural causes, and the rise since then to human activity."

Human-Produced Carbon Dioxide Contributes to Global Warming

John W. Farley

Scientific studies have shown that levels of carbon dioxide in the atmosphere have been increasing since the Industrial Revolution at the beginning of the twentieth century. John W. Farley argues in the following viewpoint that this and other scientific data have confirmed that human-released greenhouse gases, particularly CO_2, are responsible for current increases in global warming. Farley outlines the significance of the role of CO_2 in the greenhouse effect and contends that it is surprising that the increased levels of CO_2 have not resulted in greater climate change. John W. Farley is a professor of physics at the University of Nevada, Las Vegas.

John W. Farley, "The Scientific Case for Modern Anthropogenic Global Warming," *Monthly Review*, vol. 60, July/August 2008, pp. 69–75. Copyright © 2008 by MR Press. Reproduced by permission of Monthly Review Foundation.

As you read, consider the following questions:

1. Farley believes that humans have had an impact on global climate for how many years?

2. What does Farley identify to be the main sources of carbon dioxide in the atmosphere?

3. According to Farley, what is the real surprise about global warming?

When sunlight strikes the earth, infrared radiation is emitted by the earth. Greenhouse gases in the atmosphere absorb this radiation, which results in a warming of the earth. The greenhouse effect is a very large effect: without greenhouse gases in the atmosphere, the earth's surface would likely be below the freezing point of water. Carbon dioxide (CO_2) in the atmosphere has been increasing since the Industrial Revolution began, due primarily to the burning of fossil fuels and to deforestation. This increase in greenhouse gases causes an enhanced greenhouse effect, which warms the earth.

A straightforward calculation reveals that when the CO_2 in the atmosphere reaches twice the pre-industrial level, the enhanced greenhouse effect alone (i.e., neglecting any response by the earth to the enhanced greenhouse effect) will warm the earth by 1.2 to 1.3°C. There is no significant controversy among scientists about this part of global warming.

The earth will in fact respond to the increased temperature. This is called "feedback." There is controversy about the magnitude of the feedback. Analysis that takes feedback into account predicts global warming in the range of 1.5 to 4.5°C (as indicated by the Intergovernmental Panel on Climate Change [IPCC]). Controversies among climate scientists concern the magnitude of the warming, not whether or not it is occurring.

Climate is controlled by a number of factors, including changes in the earth's orbit, possibly solar variability, possibly volcanoes, and the greenhouse effect. All but the last factor are entirely natural. Human activities are not the only contribution to the greenhouse effect. Until the last two centuries, humanity had a negligible effect on climate, and all climate change was naturally occurring. Some climate changes in the distant past have been very large (e.g., ice ages) and were not caused by humans. None of these statements refute the proposition that human activities (particularly burning fossil fuels) are an important contribution to the global warming that is occurring right now. . . .

Evidence of the Greenhouse Effect

The greenhouse effect warms the earth. The warming power of the sun is mostly in the visible and ultraviolet region of the spectrum. The surface of the earth re-radiates solar energy back toward space in the form of infrared light. Because of greenhouse gases in it, the atmosphere is transparent to the visible light coming from the sun, but opaque at many wavelengths in the infrared band, resulting in the trapping of thermal energy and the warming of the earth. This is the so-called greenhouse effect, which has been known for two centuries. The first scientist to realize that the atmosphere warms the earth may have been the French mathematician and physicist Joseph Fourier in the 1820s (who should not be confused with the journalist and utopian socialist Charles Fourier). The primary greenhouse gases are water vapor, CO_2, and methane (natural gas, CH_4). I don't know any scientist who doubts that the greenhouse effect is a real effect.

Too many people fail to appreciate how large the greenhouse effect really is. A simple calculation based on the Stefan-Boltzmann law shows that if there were no greenhouse gases in the atmosphere (and if nothing else about the earth changed as a result of removing the greenhouse gases), the average surface temperature of the earth would be -18°C (-1°F), which is below the freezing point of water.

The actual observed average surface temperature of the earth is 15°C (59°F). Thus the greenhouse effect raises the earth's surface temperature by 33°C (60°F). In this sense, global warming has already happened! Not only is the greenhouse effect a real effect, it is a *large* effect.

Data Show an Intensifying Greenhouse Effect

The greenhouse effect is intensifying as a result of the greenhouse gases building up in the atmosphere due primarily to CO_2 from the burning of fossil fuels (coal, oil, and natural gas) and deforestation. Accurate data by direct experimental measurement was not available until 1959, when the geochemist C.D. Keeling started taking data at Mauna Loa, Hawaii. That measurement program has continued up to the present. . . .

The data show a seasonal cycle that matches the growing season in the Northern Hemisphere, with a maximum in May and a minimum in October. Most significant is a long-term upward trend: from 315 ppm [parts per million] in 1958 to 387 ppm in 2008. While other aspects of global warming have been controversial, nobody has ever doubted the data from this measurement program. The data are rock solid. Several research teams have measured the atmospheric CO_2 concentrations and the data from the different researchers are in agreement.

Although the earliest data from direct measurement of CO_2 in the atmosphere are from 1958, it is possible to extend the data earlier by examining air bubbles trapped in ice in Antarctica and Greenland. Data on the long-term CO_2 trend show that the CO_2 level remained stable around 280 ppm during the last 10,000 years. Then CO_2 began to rise around the time of the Industrial Revolution, and is now 38 percent higher than pre-industrial levels. Climate scientists attribute

The Identification of Carbon Dioxide as a Greenhouse Gas

Like many Victorian natural philosophers, John Tyndall was fascinated by a great variety of questions. While he was preparing an important treatise on "Heat as a Mode of Motion" [in 1863] he took time to consider geology. Tyndall had hands-on knowledge of the subject, for he was an ardent Alpinist (in 1861 he made the first ascent of the Weisshorn). Familiar with glaciers, he had been convinced by the evidence—hotly debated among scientists of his day—that tens of thousands of years ago, colossal layers of ice had covered all of northern Europe. How could climate possibly change so radically? . . .

Tyndall set out to find whether there was . . . any gas in the atmosphere that could trap heat rays. In 1859, his careful laboratory work identified several gases that did just that. The most important was simple water vapor (H_2O). Also effective was carbon dioxide (CO_2), although in the atmosphere the gas is only a few parts in ten thousand. Just as a sheet of paper will block more light than an entire pool of clear water, so the trace of CO_2 altered the balance of heat radiation through the entire atmosphere.

Spencer Weart, "The Carbon Dioxide Greenhouse Effect," The Discovery of Global Warming, June 2006. www.aip.org

the pre-industrial level of CO_2 (280 ppm) to natural causes, and the rise since then to human activity, primarily due to the aforementioned causes.

Assessing the Impact of Greenhouse Gases

The question naturally arises, what will be the effect of increased greenhouse gases? Since the greenhouse effect is a real effect, it is hard to avoid the conclusion that the buildup of greenhouse gases will result in an intensified greenhouse effect, resulting in increased global warming to some extent. In other words, the argument is over the amount of increased global warming, not over whether or not it is occurring. The amount of increased global warming might be small or large, but it is a real effect. The important scientific question is whether or not increased global warming will be large enough to cause a problem.

To answer this question, we need to understand in more detail how greenhouse gases absorb light in the infrared band. Different gases absorb light of different wavelengths. Measurements from outside the earth's atmosphere by a satellite show that CO_2 has a particularly strong absorption of light around wavelengths of 15 micrometers. [NASA climatologist] Gavin Schmidt in 2005, following work done by [climatologists] Ramanathan and Coakley in 1978, calculated the effect of greenhouse gases in the following way: If you remove one gas from the atmosphere, while keeping all the other gases constant, what is the resulting percentage change in the infrared power that is absorbed by the atmosphere? . . .

The data . . . were computed by assuming that one gas is removed from the atmosphere, leaving everything else unchanged. But since there is overlapping infrared absorption, the absorption from one species will interact with the absorption from another species. Some wavelengths of infrared light are absorbed by *both* water vapor *and* CO_2. At these overlapping regions, if you remove water vapor alone (leaving the CO_2), the CO_2 will absorb the infrared light, while if you remove CO_2 from the atmosphere (leaving the water vapor), the water vapor will absorb the infrared light. Thus the absorption by one species depends on what other species are present in the atmosphere. This accounts for the otherwise puzzling fact that the numbers do not add up linearly: If you remove all water vapor from the atmosphere, the infrared absorption will decrease by 36 percent. If you remove all greenhouse gases (and clouds) and leave only water vapor, the infrared absorption will decrease by 34 percent. The two do not add up to 100 percent, because of overlaps.

Comparing Carbon Dioxide to Water Vapor

All this is valuable background for the crucial question: How important is CO_2 in the greenhouse effect? If you remove all the CO_2 from the atmosphere, the infrared absorption decreases by 9 percent. If you remove all the greenhouse gases (including clouds) from the atmosphere *except* CO_2, the absorption decreases by 74 percent, meaning that 26 percent (= 100 percent − 74 percent) of the absorption is still present if CO_2 were the only greenhouse gas in the atmosphere. So the effect of CO_2 can be either 9 percent or 26 percent of the greenhouse effect, depending on how it is defined. Undoubtedly the different definitions account, in part, for the different values cited in the literature for the importance of CO_2 in the greenhouse effect. But whether it is 9 percent or 26 percent, the effect of CO_2 is not a negligible effect.

For water vapor, [the percent change in infrared absorption is] 36 percent and 66 percent (= 100 − 34), depending on the definition. ... The water vapor contribution to the greenhouse effect is 36 to 66 percent, while the contribution of CO_2 is 9 to 26 percent, depending on the definition. Taking the first numbers, water vapor is more important by a factor of 36/9 = 4.0, and taking the second numbers, water vapor is more important by a factor of 66/26 = 2.5. Note that water vapor is somewhat more important than CO_2, but CO_2 is by no means negligible.

Global Warming Should Be Much Greater

Let's ask what the result would be if the greenhouse gases in the atmosphere were to double. A naïve (and incorrect) calculation would be the following: Since the existing level of greenhouse gases resulted in a temperature increase of 33°C (60°F) compared to a hypothetical earth without greenhouse gases, then doubling of all the greenhouse gases would result in an additional increase of 33°C (60°F), giving an average surface temperature of the earth of 48°C (119°F). Fortunately, this frightening result stems from a misunderstanding of how greenhouse gases retain heat. The prediction of the IPCC is that doubling the level of CO_2 will result in a temperature increase of a few degrees Celsius. It is at first glance surprising and welcome that the forecasted effects of global warming are smaller than this naïve calculation would expect.

This naïve calculation is incorrect for two reasons. First, the effect of *saturation*. The atmosphere is already opaque in parts of the infrared spectrum. Increasing the level of greenhouse gases will not make any difference at those parts of the spectrum. If the absorption at a certain wavelength is close to 100 percent, doubling the CO_2 level will not double the greenhouse effect. For example, suppose that at a certain wavelength, 90 percent of the infrared light from the earth is absorbed by CO_2 in today's atmosphere. If the concentration of CO_2 in the atmosphere were doubled, the absorption cannot go to 180 percent, which is an impossibility, but will go instead to nearly 100 percent.

Second, the effect of *spectral overlap*. The absorption of infrared light by water vapor has areas of overlap with the absorption by CO_2. In regions where infrared light is already strongly absorbed by water vapor, changing the concentration of CO_2 will make little or no difference. These two effects (saturation and spectral overlap) explain why naïvely adding the effects of greenhouse gases is not correct, and overestimates the effect of increased greenhouse gases on the transmission of the atmosphere.

An increasing concentration of CO_2 will have little effect at the center of a strong absorption peak, because the atmosphere is opaque there already. Instead, an increasing concentration of CO_2 will have its largest effect on the wings of a strong peak. The atmosphere is opaque in some parts of the infrared, with "windows" where the atmosphere is transparent or partially transparent. The effect of increasing concentrations of CO_2 is to close the windows.

Although this naïve calculation is mistaken, it illustrates an important point. People are often surprised at the thought that CO_2, present in the atmosphere at only a few hundred parts per million, can result in a large enough change in the earth's average temperature to make a difference. Instead, the real surprise is that global warming is as *small* as it is.

"The view that nature was in some sort of preferred, yet fragile, state of balance before humans came along is arbitrary and philosophical—even religious."

Human-Produced Carbon Dioxide Does Not Contribute Significantly to Global Warming

Roy Spencer

In the viewpoint that follows, Roy Spencer critiques the widely accepted claim that human-produced carbon dioxide negatively impacts the planet and causes global warming. Spencer argues that scientific research has not substantiated assertions of anthropogenic, or human-caused, global warming. He contends that those scientists who preach this view have moved away from true scientific inquiry and toward a religious reverence for nature, which ultimately clouds their perception and ability to critically analyze the current environmental situation. Roy Spencer is a former NASA climate scientist and he is currently Principal Research Scientist at the University of Alabama in Huntsville; he is the author of the book Climate Confusion: How

Roy Spencer, "More Carbon Dioxide, Please: Raising a Scientific Question," *National Review Online*, May 1, 2008. Reproduced by permission.

Global Warming Hysteria Leads to Bad Science, Pandering Politicians, and Misguided Policies that Hurt the Poor.

As you read, consider the following questions:

1. What does Spencer argue to be the positive effects of increased levels of carbon dioxide (CO_2) on plants?

2. According to Spencer, what percentage of manmade CO_2 does the biosphere remove from the atmosphere every year?

3. To what destructive natural event does the author compare human production of CO_2?

There seems to be an unwritten assumption among environmentalists—and among the media—that any influence humans have on nature is, by definition, bad. I even see it in scientific papers written by climate researchers. For instance, if we can measure some minute amount of a trace gas in the atmosphere at the South Pole, well removed from its human source, we are astonished at the far-reaching effects of mankind's "pollution."

But if nature was left undisturbed, would it be any happier and more peaceful? Would the carnivores stop eating those poor, defenseless herbivores, as well as each other? Would fish and other kinds of sea life stop infringing on the rights of others by feasting on them? Would there be no more droughts, hurricanes, floods, heat waves, tornadoes, or glaciers flowing toward the sea?

In the case of global warming, the alleged culprit—carbon dioxide [CO_2]—just happens to be necessary for life on Earth. How can [environmental activist and former vice president] Al Gore say with a straight face that we are treating the atmosphere like an "open sewer" by dumping carbon dioxide into it? Would he say the same thing if we were dumping more oxygen into the atmosphere? Or more nitrogen?

The Origins of Human-Caused Global Warming Theory

The notion of human-caused global warming has its origins in late-nineteenth-century speculation about the causes of past climate shifts, especially the ice ages when large parts of North America and Europe were under kilometres of ice. Svante Arrhenius of Sweden argued that intermittent volcanic activity, and the injection of huge amounts of carbon dioxide into the atmosphere, had regulated retreats and advances of glaciations, but this theory has now been discarded. . . . Nevertheless, speculation linking potential global warming to the burning of fossil fuels, based on Arrhenius' theory, continued through the middle twentieth century.

During the 1960s and 1970s computer modelling was being developed to advance weather prediction. As they advanced, weather prediction models were adapted to crudely simulate climate, and a number of simple "what if?" experiments were carried out. For example, what would happen to Earth's temperature if the concentration of carbon dioxide in the atmosphere was doubled, or trebled [tripled]? Some of these crude experiments suggested that increased carbon dioxide might significantly raise the temperature of the earth.

As a consequence of the early modelling experiments, the issue of dangerous human-caused global warming was a consistent underlying theme of a series of international and intergovernmental environmental conferences that preceded the formation of the United Nations Environment Program (UNEP) in the early 1970s.

William Kininmonth, "Illusions of Climate Science,"
Quadrant Online, *www.quadrant.org.au*

Unsubstantiated Fears of Manmade Global Warming

As a climate researcher, I am increasingly convinced that most of our recent global warming has been natural, not manmade. If true, this would mean that global temperatures can be expected to peak in the coming years (if they haven't already), and global cooling will eventually ensue.

Just for the sake of argument, let us assume that manmade global warming really is a false alarm. In that case, we would still need to ask: What are the other negative effects of pumping more CO_2 into the atmosphere?

Well, plant physiologists have known for a long time that most vegetation loves more carbon dioxide. It grows faster, is more drought-tolerant, and is more efficient in its water use. While the pre-industrial CO_2 concentration of the atmosphere was only about 280 parts per million (ppm) by volume, and now it is around 380 ppm, some greenhouses pump it all the way up to around 1,000 ppm. How can environmentalists claim that helping vegetation to grow is a bad thing?

The bigger concern has been the possible effect of the extra CO_2 on the world's oceans, because more CO_2 lowers the pH of seawater. While it is claimed that this makes the water more acidic, this is misleading. Since seawater has a pH around 8.1, it will take an awful lot of CO_2 for it even to make the water neutral (pH=7), let alone acidic (pH less than 7).

Still, the main worry has been that the extra CO_2 could hurt the growth of plankton, which represents the start of the oceanic food chain. But recent research (published on April 18 [2008] in *Science Express*) has now shown, contrary to expectations, that one of the most common forms of plankton actually grows faster and bigger when more CO_2 is pumped into the water. Like vegetation on land, it loves the extra CO_2, too!

Increased CO_2 Levels May Benefit the Earth

It is quite possible that the biosphere (vegetation, sea life, etc.) has been starved for atmospheric CO_2. Before humans started burning fossil fuels, vegetation and ocean plankton had been gobbling up as much CO_2 out of the atmosphere as they could, but it was like a vacuum cleaner trying to suck through a stopped-up hose.

Now, no matter how much CO_2 we pump into the atmosphere each year, the biosphere takes out an average of 50 percent of that extra amount. Even after we triple the amount of CO_2 we produce, nature still takes out 50 percent of the extra amount.

I think it is time for scientists to consider the possibility that more CO_2 in the atmosphere might, on the whole, be good for life on Earth. Oh, I'm sure there will be some species which are hurt more than helped, but this is true of any change in nature. There are always winners and losers.

For instance, during a strong El Niño event, trillions of animals in the ocean die as the usual patterns of ocean temperature are disrupted. When Mother Nature does something like this it is considered natural. Yet, if humans were to do such a thing, it would be considered an environmental catastrophe. Does anyone else see something wrong with this picture?

Reassessing the Impact of Human Produced CO_2

The view that nature was in some sort of preferred, yet fragile, state of balance before humans came along is arbitrary and philosophical—even religious. It is entirely possible that there are other, more preferable states of balance in nature which are more robust and less fragile than whatever the state of nature was before we came along.

You would think that science is the last place you would find such religious opinions, yet they dominate the worldview of scientists. Natural scientists tend to worship nature, and they then teach others to worship nature, too . . . all under the guise of "science."

And to the extent that this view is religious, then making environmental laws based upon that view could be considered a violation of the establishment of religion clause of the First Amendment to the Constitution.

The automatic assumption that mankind's production of CO_2 by burning of fossil fuels is bad for the environment needs to be critically examined. Unfortunately, scientists who question that point of view are immediately branded as shills for Big Oil.

But since I am already accused of this (falsely, I might add), I really don't mind being one of the first scientists to raise the issue.

"Methane is about 20 times more powerful as a greenhouse gas than carbon dioxide and many scientists fear that its release could accelerate global warming."

Melting Permafrost Contributes to Global Warming

Steve Connor

In the following viewpoint, Steve Connor, science editor for the British daily newspaper The Independent *reports on the impact of the increasing levels of methane gas being released in the Siberian arctic. Connor notes that methane is a more dangerous greenhouse gas than carbon dioxide with greater potential to increase the rate of global warming due to its physical properties. According to Connor, scientists studying the region and measuring levels of methane there are concerned that the swelling concentration of this gas in the atmosphere will contribute to a cycle of continued global warming in which release of the gas will cause climate increases which will in turn result in the release of more methane and greater climate change.*

As you read, consider the following questions:

1. According to Connor, to what catastrophic events have scientists linked past, sudden releases of methane gas?

2. What are the current conditions the scientists in the Arctic identify as causes for the increased concentrations of methane?

3. How much methane do scientists estimate to be stored beneath the Arctic?

The first evidence that millions of tons of a greenhouse gas 20 times more potent than carbon dioxide is being released into the atmosphere from beneath the Arctic seabed has been discovered by scientists.

The Independent has been passed details of preliminary findings suggesting that massive deposits of sub-sea methane are bubbling to the surface as the Arctic region becomes warmer and its ice retreats.

A Greenhouse Gas More Powerful than Carbon Dioxide

Underground stores of methane are important because scientists believe their sudden release has in the past been responsible for rapid increases in global temperatures, dramatic changes to the climate, and even the mass extinction of species. Scientists aboard a research ship that has sailed the entire length of Russia's northern coast have discovered intense concentrations of methane—sometimes at up to 100 times background levels—over several areas covering thousands of square miles of the Siberian continental shelf.

The researchers have seen areas of sea foaming with gas bubbling up through "methane chimneys" rising from the sea floor. They believe that the sub-sea layer of permafrost, which has acted like a "lid" to prevent the gas from escaping, has melted away to allow methane to rise from underground deposits formed before the last ice age.

They have warned that this is likely to be linked with the rapid warming that the region has experienced in recent years.

Methane is about 20 times more powerful as a greenhouse gas than carbon dioxide and many scientists fear that its release could accelerate global warming in a giant positive feedback where more atmosphere methane causes higher temperatures, leading to further permafrost melting and the release of yet more methane.

The amount of methane stored beneath the Arctic is calculated to be greater than the total amount of carbon locked up in global coal reserves so there is intense interest in the stability of these deposits as the region warms at a faster rate than other places on earth.

High Levels of Methane

Orjan Gustafsson of Stockholm University in Sweden, one of the leaders of the expedition, described the scale of the methane emissions in an email exchange [in September 2008] sent from the Russian research ship *Jacob Smirnitskyi*.

"We had a hectic finishing of the sampling programme yesterday and this past night," said Dr Gustafsson. "An extensive area of intense methane release was found. At earlier sites we had found elevated levels of dissolved methane. Yesterday, for the first time, we documented a field where the release was so intense that the methane did not have time to dissolve into the seawater but was rising as methane bubbles to the sea surface. These 'methane chimneys' were documented on echo sounder and with seismic [instruments]."

At some locations, methane concentrations reached 100 times background levels. These anomalies have been seen in the East Siberian Sea and the Laptev Sea, covering several tens of thousands of square kilometres, amounting to millions of tons of methane, said Dr Gustafsson. "This may be of the

Methane: More Information Is Needed

Over the last few years atmospheric methane concentrations have hardly changed. This is clearly good news for those worried about continued greenhouse warming, but until scientists understand why, there is no assurance that increased emissions won't resume. This stands as a clear reminder that we still do not know everything we need to about methane. Many of the anthropogenic [human] sources of methane such as irrigation, mining, farm practices, etc. are however relatively cheap and straightforward to control. For example, New Zealand's primary contribution to greenhouse gas emissions is from sheep digestive processes, and scientists there are experimenting with changes to feed that have the potential to reduce methane production enormously. Similarly, improved capture of methane released in mining and oil operations is providing a cleaner fuel source and increasing profits for the companies concerned. . . .

Over the last 30 years, methane has gone from being a gas of no importance, to—in some researchers' eyes, at least—possibly the most important greenhouse gas both for understanding climate change and as a cost-effective target for future emission reductions. Whether some of these new ideas stand up to the scrutiny of the wider climate research community remains to be seen, but one thing is certain, the scientific journey of methane is not yet complete.

Gavin Schmidt, "Methane:
A Scientific Journey from Obscurity to Climate Super-Stardom,"
NASA GISS, September 2004. www.giss.nasa

same magnitude as presently estimated from the global ocean," he said. "Nobody knows how many more such areas exist on the extensive East Siberian continental shelves.

"The conventional thought has been that the permafrost 'lid' on the sub-sea sediments on the Siberian shelf should cap and hold the massive reservoirs of shallow methane deposits in place. The growing evidence for release of methane in this inaccessible region may suggest that the permafrost lid is starting to get perforated and thus leak methane . . . The permafrost now has small holes. We have found elevated levels of methane above the water surface and even more in the water just below. It is obvious that the source is the seabed."

Recent Environmental Changes

The preliminary findings of the International Siberian Shelf Study 2008, being prepared for publication by the American Geophysical Union, are being overseen by Igor Semiletov of the Far-Eastern branch of the Russian Academy of Sciences. Since 1994, he has led about 10 expeditions in the Laptev Sea but during the 1990s he did not detect any elevated levels of methane. However, since 2003 he reported a rising number of methane "hotspots," which have now been confirmed using more sensitive instruments on board the *Jacob Smirnitskyi*.

Dr Semiletov has suggested several possible reasons why methane is now being released from the Arctic, including the rising volume of relatively warmer water being discharged from Siberia's rivers due to the melting of the permafrost on the land.

The Arctic region as a whole has seen a 4 [degrees Celsius] rise in average temperatures over recent decades and a dramatic decline in the area of the Arctic Ocean covered by summer sea ice. Many scientists fear that the loss of sea ice could accelerate the warming trend because open ocean soaks up more heat from the sun than the reflective surface of an ice-covered sea.

"*Scientists say one day's deforestation is equivalent to the carbon footprint of eight million people flying to New York.*"

Deforestation Contributes to Global Warming

Daniel Howden

Daniel Howden argues in the following viewpoint that among the many factors causing global warming, deforestation has a more severe impact than many other human activities. Howden states that deforestation is the only activity in developing countries, such as Brazil and Indonesia, that could place them just behind the United States and China in terms of greenhouse gas emissions. He cites the advice of numerous scientists and reports calling for swift action to end deforestation. Daniel Howden is a regular contributor to the London based newspaper The Independent.

As you read, consider the following questions:

1. According to the Global Canopy Programme, deforestation accounts for what percentage of global emissions of heat-trapping gases?

2. What are some of the countries Howden identifies as being leaders in carbon emissions caused by deforestation?

3. According to Howden, what percent of all life on earth lives in tropical forests, and what percent of the earth's surface do these forests cover?

The accelerating destruction of the rainforests that form a precious cooling band around the Earth's equator, is now being recognised as one of the main causes of climate change. Carbon emissions from deforestation far outstrip damage caused by planes and automobiles and factories.

The rampant slashing and burning of tropical forests is second only to the energy sector as a source of greenhouse gases according to a report published today by the Oxford-based Global Canopy Programme an alliance of leading rainforest scientists.

Figures from the GCP, summarising the latest findings from the United Nations, and building on estimates contained in the Stern Report, show deforestation accounts for up to 25 per cent of global emissions of heat-trapping gases, while transport and industry account for 14 per cent each; and aviation makes up only 3 per cent of the total.

"Tropical forests are the elephant in the living room of climate change," said Andrew Mitchell, the head of the GCP.

Scientists say one day's deforestation is equivalent to the carbon footprint of eight million people flying to New York. Reducing those catastrophic emissions can be achieved most quickly and most cheaply by halting the destruction in Brazil, Indonesia, the Congo and elsewhere.

No new technology is needed, says the GCP, just the political will and a system of enforcement and incentives that makes the trees worth more to governments and individuals standing than felled. "The focus on technological fixes for the emissions of rich nations while giving no incentive to poorer nations to stop burning the standing forest means we are putting the cart before the horse," said Mr Mitchell.

Most people think of forests only in terms of the CO_2 they absorb. The rainforests of the Amazon, the Congo basin and Indonesia are thought of as the lungs of the planet. But the destruction of those forests will in the next four years alone, in the words of Sir Nicholas Stern, pump more CO_2 into the atmosphere than every flight in the history of aviation to at least 2025.

Indonesia became the third-largest emitter of greenhouse gases in the world. Following close behind is Brazil. Neither nation has heavy industry on a comparable scale with the EU, India or Russia and yet they comfortably outstrip all other countries, except the United States and China.

What both countries do have in common is tropical forest that is being cut and burned with staggering swiftness. Smoke stacks visible from space climb into the sky above both countries, while satellite images capture similar destruction from the Congo basin, across the Democratic Republic of Congo, the Central African Republic and the Republic of Congo.

According to the latest audited figures from 2003, two billion tons of CO_2 enters the atmosphere every year from deforestation. That destruction amounts to 50 million acres—or an area the size of England, Wales and Scotland felled annually.

The remaining standing forest is calculated to contain 1,000 billion tons of carbon, or double what is already in the atmosphere.

As the GCP's report concludes: "If we lose forests, we lose the fight against climate change."

Standing forest was not included in the original Kyoto protocols and stands outside the carbon markets that the report from the Panel on Climate Change (IPCC) pointed to this month as the best hope for halting catastrophic warming.

The landmark Stern Report, and the influential McKinsey Report in January agreed that forests offer the "single largest opportunity for cost-effective and immediate reductions of carbon emissions."

International demand has driven intensive agriculture, logging and ranching that has proved an inexorable force for deforestation; conservation has been no match for commerce. The leading rainforest scientists are now calling for the immediate inclusion of standing forests in internationally regulated carbon markets that could provide cash incentives to halt this disastrous process.

Forestry experts and policy makers have been meeting in Bonn, Germany, this week to try to put deforestation on top of the agenda for the UN climate summit in Bali, Indonesia, this year. Papua New Guinea, among the world's poorest nations, last year declared it would have no choice but to continue deforestation unless it was given financial incentives to do otherwise.

Richer nations already recognise the value of uncultivated land. The EU offers €200 (£135) per hectare subsidies for "environmental services" to its farmers to leave their land unused.

And yet there is no agreement on placing a value on the vastly more valuable land in developing countries. More than 50 per cent of the life on Earth is in tropical forests, which cover less than 7 per cent of the planet's surface.

They generate the bulk of rainfall worldwide and act as a thermostat for the Earth. Forests are also home to 1.6 billion of the world's poorest people who rely on them for subsistence. However, forest experts say governments continue to pursue science fiction solutions to the coming climate catastrophe, preferring bio-fuel subsidies, carbon capture schemes and next-generation power stations.

Putting a price on the carbon these vital forests contain is the only way to slow their destruction. Hylton Philipson, a trustee of Rainforest Concern, explained: "In a world where we are witnessing a mounting clash between food security, energy security and environmental security—while there's money to be made from food and energy and no income to be derived from the standing forest, it's obvious that the forest will take the hit."

> *"It is too bad that those who are looking for ways to reduce their climate change footprint usually are not informed about the animal food–global warming connection."*

Livestock Agriculture Contributes to Global Warming

Marisa Miller Wolfson

Marisa Miller Wolfson is the director of outreach at Kind Green Planet, an organization dedicated to promoting healthy, humane, eco-friendly living through grassroots educational programs. In the viewpoint that follows, Wolfson argues that the production of animal food products accounts for the largest percentage of human-released greenhouse gases in the atmosphere. She cites numerous reports and studies linking animal agriculture to the increasing atmospheric levels of methane and nitrous oxide. Further, she contends that these gases are greater contributors to global warming than carbon dioxide. Wolfson worries that if humans worldwide continue consuming meat at in-

creasing rates and do not alter their dietary practices soon, animal agriculture will have an irreversible impact on the global climate.

As you read, consider the following questions:

1. According to the author, what percentage of fossil fuel use was related to food production?

2. What percentage of methane and nitrous oxide emissions does the author attribute to livestock?

3. According to Wolfson, how much has per capita consumption of meat increased in the past 50 years, and why does she believe this trend of increased global meat consumption is likely to continue?

Al Gore's Oscar-winning documentary, *An Inconvenient Truth*, garnered a windstorm of media attention that likely sent people scurrying for fluorescent light bulbs to curb their carbon dioxide emissions, but some scientists have argued that the film does not paint a complete picture of the real causes of climate change, and it leaves out the most inconvenient truth of all: the connection between global warming and the steak knife.

Just four months before former Vice Pres. Gore gave his Academy Award acceptance speech, the United Nations Food and Agriculture Organization published a report that identified the number-one contributor to global warming. It was not transportation or power plants; it was livestock. Entitled *Livestock's Long Shadow*, the report barely made a blip on the media's radar, perhaps because it uncovered a truth that was too inconvenient for most Americans, even Gore, to swallow. As a result, the American public missed out on one very effective strategy to combat climate change.

Fossil Fuels and Food Production

The livestock-global warming connection is nothing new to the scientific community. As *An Inconvenient Truth* was nearing its theatrical release in the spring of 2006, an issue of the journal *Earth Interactions* published a piece by Gidon Eschel and Pamela A. Martin from the Department of Geophysical Sciences at the University of Chicago. The assistant professors had conducted a study of the energy consumption and greenhouse gas emissions associated with food production. In their report, they point out that production of food in the U.S. requires increasingly more energy. In 2002, for example, 17% of all the fossil fuel used in the U.S. went into food production, and that percentage rises by an average of one percent per year. Burning these fossil fuels emits more than three-quarters of a ton of carbon dioxide [CO_2] per person.

To find out which types of foods require the most fossil fuels and, as a result, release the most CO_2, they considered five different diets. Each equaled 3,774 calories a day, and ranged from the average American diet to red meat, fish, poultry, and vegetarian diets. It came as no surprise to the researchers that the vegetarian diet ranked number one as the most energy-efficient, followed by poultry and the average American diet. It did come as a surprise, however, that fish almost was on a par with red meat as the least efficient—a large amount of fossil fuel is necessary for long-distance voyages to catch large predatory fishes such as tuna and swordfish. Moreover, salmon farming is not energy efficient.

To translate these results into everyday action, it would mean that, in order to curb the use of fossil fuels and the subsequent emission of CO_2 that results from their combustion, one need only adopt a vegan diet.

Livestock Generate the Most Powerful Greenhouse Gases

Livestock's Long Shadow, meanwhile, outlines livestock's "enormous" contribution to climate change. Most people who have read the report were shocked to learn that 18% of the current global warming effect can be attributed to livestock—an even larger contribution than the transportation sector worldwide. Only nine percent of total carbon dioxide emissions are generated by livestock, but 37% of methane emissions and 65% of nitrous oxide—two powerful greenhouse gases—come from livestock. Moreover, some scientists would argue that it actually is the more potent non-carbon dioxide greenhouse gases that are responsible for most of the global warming the world has experienced thus far.

In his report, *A New Global Warming Strategy* published by Earth Save International, physicist Noam Mohr refers to data by James Hansen, the "grandfather of the global warming theory." As director of NASA's Goddard Institute for Space Studies, Hansen has been quoted by Gore as well as other environmentalists, and is known as a man of sound science by global warming gurus such as James McCarthy, co-chair of the [Intergovernmental] Panel on Climate Change's Working Group II. Hansen's data suggest that many CO_2 emissions actually cool the atmosphere as well as warm it. To be specific, when cars and power plants—the primary sources of carbon dioxide emissions—release the gas, they simultaneously emit aerosols, which have a temporary cooling effect. These cancel out the warming of CO_2, at least for the short term. For that reason, Mohr claims, most of the global warming we have seen up until now—and that we will witness in the near future—might not, in fact, be from the carbon dioxide emitted by cars and power plants.

You probably will not hear this information from environmental activists, though, because they would not want to give industries any excuse to lower regulations on CO_2 emissions. Furthermore, because the aerosols' cooling effect merely is temporary, CO_2 must be addressed for the long term. However, if predictions are true that we have only a few decades before the melting polar ice caps submerge Florida into the sea, then this issue should be addressed from all angles.

Evaluating the Numbers

Much of the mass misconception about carbon dioxide has to do with numbers: humans produce more CO_2 than all of the greenhouse gases combined. However, what people might not realize is that, when it comes to global warming, it is not just about quantity of greenhouse gases, it also is about quality. For instance, methane is 23 times stronger than CO_2 in its warming effects: nitrous oxide, 296 times. Even though methane is weaker than nitrous oxide, the sheer amount of it in the atmosphere makes it a devastating greenhouse gas.

Animal agriculture plays the leading role in methane emissions, according to the United Nations report. It is responsible for 35–40% of all methane generated by human activity. Animal agriculture produces more than 100,000,000 tons of methane a year, and the figure is rising. As global demand for meat increases, so does the supply. From 1950–2002, world meat production went from 44,000,000 to 242,000,000 tons a year. Not only is the higher population driving the demand, people are consuming more meat individually. In the past 50 years alone, per capita consumption of meat has increased from 17 to 39 kilograms per person. As countries such as China and India adopt a more Western diet, demand for meat is rising rapidly, driving predictions that global meat consumption will double again by 2020.

To compare which animal foods are the worst offenders, Eschel and Martin estimated that 56% of all non-CO_2 greenhouse gas emissions come from beef, 29% from dairy, and 15% from pork. This includes enteric fermentation, manure management, and nitrous oxide manure management. Most of the methane that is produced in animal agriculture comes from the digestive process of livestock, and most of that does not originate from the rear end of the animal, as one might expect, but rather from the front end during the benign act of exhalation. The amount of methane emanating from one cow may seem negligible, but when you consider that a single cow

Meat Consumption and Cruelty to Humans

The climate-food discussion must be about more than just facts, more than pounds of greenhouse gases per units of food. It's got to be about morality, about right versus wrong. And I don't mean the usual morality of environmental "stewardship." Or even the issue of cruelty to farm animals. I'm talking here about cruelty to people, about the explicit harm to humans that results from meat consumption and its role as a driving force in climate change. Knowingly eating food that makes you fat or harms your local fish and birds is one thing. Knowingly eating food that makes children across much of the world hungry is another. . . .

If we in the West don't alter course in the coming years, if we allow extreme global warming to become reality, an impact on the U.S. diet could very well be a great reduction in the amount of meat on our tables—a reduction imposed on us by nature instead of achieved by us through enlightened lifestyle changes. . . .

But in the Congo and other poor countries, in places like Bangladesh and Peru and Vietnam, where meat consumption is already low, severe climate change means food off the table. It means hungry children. It means the rains don't come on time or at all in tiny villages [dependent on them for growing food crops]. It means, in the end, cruelty to people.

Mike Tidwell,
"The Low-Carbon Diet", Audubon,
January/February 2009.

can exhale 634 quarts of methane per day and then multiply that by the 1,300,000,000 cows that are in the world today, it is not hard to see why this matter should be taken seriously.

Controlling Methane Pollution

The initial production of methane that comes from digestion (85%) is followed by an additional emission (15%) from massive "lagoons," a euphemism for cess-pits of untreated farm animal waste. To get a sense of exactly how much waste we are talking about, consider that farm animals produce 500,000,000 tons of manure annually. That is three times more raw waste than is made by U.S. citizens, according to USDA [United States Department of Agriculture] figures. Waste disposal becomes problematic when the manure in the lagoons leaches into ground and surface water or spills directly into lakes, streams, and rivers. In fact, the Environmental Protection Agency estimates that chicken, hog, and cattle excrement has polluted 35,000 miles of rivers in 22 states and contaminated groundwater in 17 states.

Moreover, the amount of methane in the atmosphere has doubled since pre-industrial times. It does not help that human-produced methane stimulates the naturally produced variety. Microbial decay of organic matter in wetlands is the number-one source of natural methane. When temperatures in wetlands rise due to human-induced global warming, the organic matter in wetlands decays more, releasing even more natural methane. If we want to halt global warming in its tracks, why not reduce or eliminate the primary source of methane, the potent greenhouse gas that is causing much (if not most) of the global warming we are seeing today? Simply switching from a meat-based lifestyle to a pure vegetarian—or vegan—one is the easiest, most effective way to do this.

Not many people know that methane cycles out of the atmosphere after approximately 10 years, while CO_2 takes at least 100 years to do so. Given that the average methane-producing animal is only allowed to live for one or two years, if everyone went vegetarian today, it should take about 10 years for animal agriculture-induced methane emissions to disappear. In contrast, even if affordable, zero-emissions cars and power plants were available today, it would take much longer for them to be built and then replace the older models. Meanwhile, you can walk into any supermarket and find vegetarian food.

Advocacy for Vegetarian and Vegan Diets

It is too bad that those who are looking for ways to reduce their climate change footprint usually are not informed about the animal food–global warming connection. Environmental organizations should consider vegetarianism advocacy as a core part of their agenda and frame it in a way that people can relate to, as did Eschel and Martin in explaining that the food people eat is just as important as the type of cars they drive.

According to their data, even if you normally eat about eight percent fewer animal products than the average American, by going vegan you still can decrease you greenhouse gas emissions by the same amount as switching from a normal sedan to a hybrid—and if you eat about eight percent more animal products than the average American, by going vegan you reduce your greenhouse gas emissions by the same amount as switching from an SUV to a normal sedan. If more Americans heard the argument framed in this way, they might feel less inclined to bring their normal sedan into the drive-through at the local fast-food restaurant.

Finally, government policy should encourage vegetarian diets. Every five years, the USDA tells us what is best to eat in its *Dietary Guide for Americans*. Since 1995, when vegetarianism was mentioned for the first time by name, the guidelines have pushed people more and more towards plant foods. In 2000, the guide urged, "Use plant foods as the foundation of your meals." Then, from 2000–05, the quantity of fruits and vegetables a person should eat every day increased from 2½ to 4½ cups. The daily intake of cholesterol (found only in animal foods), on the other hand, should not exceed 300 milligrams. That is the equivalent of just two small eggs. Try telling the average American that, after consuming two eggs sunnyside up for breakfast, he or she will be cut off from animal products for the rest of the day.

It seems that the USDA already knows that plants are good for our health, so putting more vegetarian-friendly policies into place will benefit the planet's health, too. How about an environmental tax on meat like the one recommended on gasoline, or shifting farm subsidies to privilege plant agriculture over animal agriculture? Perhaps that would prompt Al Gore to overcome his own inconvenient love of burgers and produce the sequel, *Meat: An Inconvenient Food*.

Periodical Bibliography

The following articles have been selected to supplement the diverse views presented in this chapter.

Phil Berardelli — "Did Icebergs Warm the World?" *Science Now*, November 21, 2008.

Christopher Hawthorne — "Emerald Cities," *Sierra*, January/February 2009.

Andrew Monaghan — "Antarctica and Climate Change," *World Watch*, January/February 2009.

New Scientist — "Cities Not to Blame for Climate Change," October 4, 2008.

Pollution Engineering — "Are Bugs Causing Climate Change?" December 2008.

Andrew C. Revkin — "New Warnings on Climate Change," *The New York Times*, January 20, 2007.

Doyle Rice — "Studies Link Man-made Causes to Rise in Humidity," *USA Today*, October 11, 2007.

Jeff Rubin — "Life on Ice," *Audubon*, January/February 2009.

Tom Scheffelin — "Global Warming Causes Carbon Dioxide," *Design News*, November 5, 2007.

Bryan Walsh — "Unfrozen Tundra," *Time*, October 6, 2008.

Bryan Welch — "It's the Population, Kids," *Utne Reader*, January/February 2009.

OPPOSING
VIEWPOINTS®
SERIES

CHAPTER 3

What Is the Impact of Global Warming?

Chapter Preface

In an October 2007 paper, the Center for Integrative Environmental Research (CIER) at the University of Maryland looked at the impact of global warming on the environment of the United States to assess the expected costs of continued inaction. CIER anticipates that, if unchecked, global warming will lead to more wildfires in the West, claiming $1–$2 billion per large conflagration. The Plains States will likely suffer more frequent flooding and drought, leading to billions of dollars in lost agriculture, while the South will receive less precipitation and consequently face water shortages. CIER also predicts the East Coast will fall prey to rising sea levels and stronger storms that will force evacuations and destroy property to the tune of $1–$6 billion per crisis.

Beyond the price tags for response, loss, and rebuilding, though, CIER sees a multiplicity of hidden costs. The organization writes:

> Besides the replacement value of infrastructure, for example, there are real costs of re-routing traffic, workdays and productivity lost, provision of temporary shelter and supplies, potential relocation and retraining costs, and others. Likewise, the increased levels of uncertainty and risk, brought about by climate change, impose new costs on the insurance, banking, and investment industries, as well as complicate the planning processes for the agricultural and manufacturing sectors and for public works projects.

To keep up with some of these costs, CIER expects that state and local governments will have to raise taxes and pass the burden on to the public. Therefore the organization believes that acting immediately to redress climate change will prove the soundest fiscal policy if it is coupled with preparations for the "unavoidable impacts" resulting from the damage already done.

While the United States may be better prepared to bear the brunt of such an economic crisis, other nations may not. Some experts fear that Third World countries will be hit hardest, especially lowland countries like Bangladesh and Indonesia, which will lose coastlines and easily succumb to flooding. Economist Sir Nicholas Stern, a former vice president of the World Bank, has argued in a well-known report that the world economy could decline by 20 percent if global warming progresses. He predicts that 200 million people could become refugees from drought and famine in such a circumstance. But Stern remains optimistic about coordinating a united front against climate change: "We have the time and knowledge to act. But only if we act internationally, strongly and urgently."

The authors and experts in the following chapter forgo this analysis of the financial costs associated with global warming in order to examine the impacts of climate change upon wildlife, human health, and the environment. While some of these writers express concern about an impending climate crisis, others are skeptical that the costs of continued warming will be so great.

| "We are entering a new era, a period of rapid and often unpredictable climate change."

Global Warming Is Melting the Polar Ice Caps

Lester R. Brown

In the viewpoint that follows, Lester R. Brown, founder and president of the Earth Policy Institute, an organization dedicated to promoting a sustainable future for humans and the planet, argues that global warming is causing the polar ice caps and other glaciers around the world to melt. He presents the research of numerous scientists from across the globe who have reached the consensus that global warming is the cause of increasing ice melt worldwide. Brown further outlines the consequences of the melting ice caps, touching on both decreased agricultural production and mass displacement of people due to rising sea levels. He contends that these problems could threaten and ultimately destroy all of civilization.

Lester R. Brown, "Rising Temperatures and Rising Seas," *Plan B 3.0: Mobilizing to Save Civilization*. New York: W.W. Norton & Company, 2008. Copyright © 2008 by Earth Policy Institute. All rights reserved. Used by permission of W. W. Norton & Company, Inc.

As you read, consider the following questions:

1. Brown argues that the agriculture of which continents will be affected by the melting of mountain glaciers and ice?

2. According to Brown, what are "positive feedback loops," and how do they impact the melting ice worldwide?

3. What evidence does Brown present to suggest that the melting of the polar ice caps is increasing?

Civilization has evolved during a period of remarkable climate stability, but this era is drawing to a close. We are entering a new era, a period of rapid and often unpredictable climate change. The new climate norm is change. . . .

Today not only do we know that the earth is getting warmer, but we can begin to see some of the effects of higher temperatures. Mountain glaciers are melting almost everywhere. Himalayan glaciers that feed the rivers that irrigate the rice fields of China and the wheat fields of India are fast disappearing.

The attention of climate scientists is turning to the melting ice sheets of Greenland and West Antarctica. If we cannot cut carbon emissions quickly enough to save these, then sea level will rise 12 meters (39 feet). Many of the world's coastal cities will be under water; over 600 million coastal dwellers will be forced to move. . . .

Melting Glaciers in Asia

Snow and ice masses in mountains are nature's freshwater reservoirs—nature's way of storing water to feed rivers during the dry season. Now they are being threatened by the rise in temperature. Even a 1-degree rise in temperature in mountainous regions can markedly reduce the share of precipitation falling as snow and boost that coming down as rain. This in turn increases flooding during the rainy season and reduces the snowmelt that flows into rivers.

Beyond this, the glaciers that feed rivers during the dry season are melting. Some have disappeared entirely. Nowhere is the melting of glaciers of more concern than in Asia, where 1.3 billion people depend for their water supply on rivers originating in the Himalayan Mountains and the adjacent Tibet-Qinghai Plateau.

India's Gangotri Glacier, which supplies 70 percent of the water to the Ganges, is not only melting, it is doing so at an accelerated rate. If this melting continues to accelerate, the Gangotri's life expectancy will be measured in decades and the Ganges will become a seasonal river, flowing only during the rainy season. For the 407 million Indians and Bangladeshis who live in the Ganges basin, this could be a life-threatening loss of water.

The Impact on Glaciers in Diverse Regions

In China, which is even more dependent than India on river water for irrigation, the situation is particularly challenging. Chinese government data show the glaciers on the Tibet-Qinghai Plateau that feed both the Yellow and Yangtze Rivers are melting at 7 percent a year. The Yellow River, whose basin is home to 147 million people, could experience a large dry-season flow reduction. The Yangtze River, by far the larger of the two, is threatened by the disappearance of glaciers as well. The basin's 369 million people rely heavily on rice from fields irrigated with Yangtze River water.

Yao Tandong, a leading Chinese glaciologist, predicts that two thirds of China's glaciers could be gone by 2060. "The full-scale glacier shrinkage in the plateau region," Yao says, "will eventually lead to an ecological catastrophe."

Other Asian rivers that originate in this rooftop of the world include the Indus, with 178 million people in its basin in India and Pakistan; the Brahmaputra, which flows through Bangladesh; and the Mekong, which waters Cambodia, Laos, Thailand, and Viet Nam.

In Africa, Tanzania's snow-capped Kilimanjaro may soon be snow- and ice-free. Ohio State University glaciologist Lonnie Thompson's studies of Kilimanjaro show that Africa's tallest mountain lost 33 percent of its ice field between 1989 and 2000. He projects that its snowcap could disappear entirely by 2015. Nearby Mount Kenya has lost 7 of its 18 glaciers. Local rivers fed by these glaciers are becoming seasonal rivers, generating conflict among the 2 million people who depend on them for water supplies during the dry season.

South American Glaciers Are Disappearing

Bernard Francou, research director for the French government's Institute of Research and Development, believes that 80 percent of South American glaciers will disappear within the next 15 years. For countries like Bolivia, Ecuador, and Peru, which rely on glaciers for water for household and irrigation use, this is not good news.

Peru, which stretches some 1,600 kilometers along the vast Andean mountain range and which is home to 70 percent of the earth's tropical glaciers, is in trouble. Some 22 percent of its glacial endowment, which feeds the many Peruvian rivers that supply water to the cities in the semi-arid coastal regions, has disappeared. Lonnie Thompson reports that the Quelccaya Glacier in southern Peru, which was retreating by 6 meters per year in the 1960s, is now retreating by 60 meters annually.

Many of Peru's farmers irrigate their wheat and potatoes with the river water from these disappearing glaciers. During the dry season, farmers are totally dependent on irrigation water. For Peru's 28 million people, shrinking glaciers will eventually mean a shrinking food supply.

Lima, a city of 7 million people, gets most of its water from three rivers high in the Andes, rivers that are fed partly by glacial melt. While the glaciers are melting, the river flows are above normal, but once they are gone, the river flows will drop sharply, leaving Lima with severe water shortages.

U.S. Snowfields Are Not Immune to Effects of Climate Change

In many agricultural regions, snow and ice masses are the leading source of irrigation and drinking water. In the southwestern United States, for instance, the Colorado River—the region's primary source of irrigation water—depends on snowfields in the Rockies for much of its flow: California, in addition to depending heavily on the Colorado, also relies on snowmelt from the Sierra Nevada in the eastern part of the state. Both the Sierra Nevada and the coastal range supply irrigation water to California's Central Valley, the world's fruit and vegetable basket.

Preliminary results of an analysis of rising temperature effects on three major river systems in the western United States—the Columbia, the Sacramento, and the Colorado—indicate that the winter snow pack in the mountains feeding them will be dramatically reduced and that winter rainfall and flooding will increase.

With a business-as-usual energy policy, global climate models project a 70-percent reduction in the amount of snow pack for the western United States by mid-century. A detailed study of the Yakima River Valley, a vast fruit-growing region in Washington state, conducted by the U.S. Department of Energy's Pacific Northwest National Laboratory shows progressively heavier harvest losses as the snow pack shrinks, reducing irrigation water flows.

Agriculture Worldwide Will Suffer

Agriculture in the Central Asian countries of Afghanistan, Kazakhstan, Kyrgyzstan, Tajikistan, Turkmenistan, and Uzbekistan depends heavily on snowmelt from the Hindu Kush, Pamir, and Tien Shan mountain ranges for irrigation water. Nearby Iran gets much of its water from the snowmelt in the 5,700-meter-high Alborz Mountains between Tehran and the Caspian Sea.

The snow and ice masses in the world's leading mountain ranges and the water they store are taken for granted simply because they have been there since before agriculture began. Now that is changing. If we continue raising the earth's temperature, we risk losing the reservoirs in the sky on which cities and farmers depend.

Melting Ice Leads to Rising Seas

Ice melting in mountainous regions not only affects river flows, it also affects sea level rise. On a larger scale, the melting of the earth's two massive ice sheets—Antarctica and Greenland—could raise sea level enormously. If the Greenland ice sheet were to melt, it would raise sea level 7 meters (23 feet). Melting of the West Antarctic Ice Sheet would raise sea level 5 meters (16 feet). But even just partial melting of these ice sheets will have a dramatic effect on sea level rise. Senior scientists are noting that the IPCC [Intergovernmental Panel on Climate Change] projections of sea level rise during this century of 18 to 59 centimeters are already obsolete and that a rise of 2 meters during his time is within range.

Assessing the prospects for the Greenland ice sheet begins with looking at the warming of the Arctic region. A 2005 study, *Impacts of a Warming Arctic*, concluded that the Arctic is warming almost twice as fast as the rest of the planet. Conducted by the Arctic Climate Impact Assessment (ACIA) team, an international group of 300 scientists, the study found that in the regions surrounding the Arctic, including Alaska, western Canada, and eastern Russia, winter temperatures have already climbed by 3–4 degrees Celsius (4–7 degrees Fahrenheit) over the last half-century. Robert Corell, chair of ACIA, says this region "is experiencing some of the most rapid and severe climate change on Earth."

In testimony before the U.S. Senate Commerce Committee, Sheila Watt-Cloutier, an Inuit speaking on behalf of the 155,000 Inuits who live in Alaska, Canada, Greenland, and the

Global Warming Melts the World's Highest Ski Area

Even in better times, the Chacaltaya ski area was no competition for Aspen [a ski resort town in Colorado]. Set in a bleak valley high in the Andes mountains of Bolivia, it offered a half-mile swoop downhill, a precarious ride back up on a rope tow, and coca-leaf tea for altitude headaches. At 17,250 feet, after all, Chacaltaya was the highest ski area in the world. "It gave us a lot of glory," says Walter Laguna, the president of Bolivia's mountain club. "We organized South American championships— with Chile, with Argentina, with Colombia."

The glory days are over. Skiing at this improbable spot depended on a small glacier that made a passable ski run when Bolivia's wet season dusted it with snow. The glacier was already shrinking when the ski area opened in 1939. But in the past decade, it's gone into a death spiral.

By last year [2006] all that remained were three patches of gritty ice, the largest just a couple of hundred yards across. The rope tow traversed boulder fields. Laguna insists that skiing will go on. Perhaps the club can make artificial snow, he says; perhaps it can haul in slabs of ice to mend the glacier. But in the long run, he knows, Chacaltaya is history. "The process is irreversible. Global warming will continue."

Tim Appenzeller,
"The Big Thaw," National Geographic,
June 2007.

Russian Federation, described their struggle to survive in the fast-changing Arctic climate as "a snapshot of what is happening to the planet." She called the warming of the Arctic "a defining event in the history of this planet." And she went on to say "the Earth is literally melting."

The ACIA report described how the retreat of the sea ice has devastating consequences for polar bears, whose very survival may be at stake. A subsequent report indicated that polar bears, struggling to survive, are turning to cannibalism. Also threatened are ice-dwelling seals, a basic food source for the Inuit.

New Data Suggest the Problem Is Worsening

Since this 2005 report, there is new evidence that the problem is worse than previously thought. A team of scientists from the National Snow and Ice Data Center and the National Center for Atmospheric Research, which has compiled data on Arctic Ocean summer ice melting from 1953 to 2006, concluded that the ice is melting much faster than climate models had predicted. They found that from 1979 to 2006 the summer sea ice shrinkage accelerated to 9.1 percent a decade. In 2007, Arctic sea ice shrank some 20 percent below the previous record set in 2005. This suggests that the sea could be ice-free well before 2050, the earliest date projected by the IPCC in its 2007 report. Arctic scientist Julienne Stroeve observed that the shrinking Arctic sea ice may have reached "a tipping point that could trigger a cascade of climate change reaching into Earth's temperate regions."

Reinforcing this concern is a recent study by Joséfino Comiso, a senior scientist at NASA's Goddard Space Flight Center. Comiso reported for the first time that even the winter ice cover in the Arctic Ocean shrank by 6 percent in 2005 and again in 2006. This new development, combined with the news that the sea ice cover is thinning, provides further evidence that the ice is not recovering after its melt season, meaning that summer ice in the Arctic Ocean could disappear much sooner than earlier thought possible.

Walt Meier, a researcher at the U.S. National Snow and Ice Data Center who tracks the changes in Arctic sea ice, views the winter shrinkage with alarm. He believes there is "a good chance" that the Arctic tipping point has been reached. "People have tried to think of ways we could get back to where we were. We keep going further and further in the hole, and it's getting harder and harder to get out of it." Some scientists now think that the Arctic Ocean could be ice-free in the summer as early as 2030.

An Endless Cycle of Warming

Scientists are concerned that "positive feedback loops" may be starting to kick in. This term refers to a situation where a trend already under way begins to reinforce itself. Two of these potential feedback mechanisms are of particular concern to scientists. The first, in the Arctic, is the albedo effect. When incoming sunlight strikes the ice in the Arctic Ocean, up to 70 percent of it is reflected back into space. Only 30 percent is absorbed as heat. As the Arctic sea ice melts, however, and the incoming sunlight hits the much darker open water, only 6 percent is reflected back into space and 94 percent is converted into heat. This may account for the accelerating shrinkage of the Arctic sea ice and the rising regional temperature that directly affects the Greenland ice sheet.

If all the ice in the Arctic Ocean melts, it will not affect sea level because the ice is already in the water. But it will lead to a much warmer Arctic region as more of the incoming sunlight is absorbed as heat. This is of particular concern because Greenland lies largely within the Arctic Circle. As the Arctic region warms, the island's ice sheet—up to 1.6 kilometers (1 mile) thick in places—is beginning to melt.

The second positive feedback mechanism also has to do with ice melting. What scientists once thought was a fairly simple linear process—that is, a certain amount at the surface of an ice sheet melts each year, depending on the temperature—is now seen to be much more complicated. As the surface ice begins to melt, some of the water filters down through cracks in the glacier, lubricating the surface between the glacier and the rock beneath it. This accelerates the glacial flow and the calving [breaking off] of icebergs into the surrounding ocean. The relatively warm water flowing through the glacier also carries surface heat deep inside the ice sheet far faster than it would otherwise penetrate by simple conduction.

Troubling New Data

Several recent studies report that the melting of the Greenland ice sheet is accelerating. A study published in *Science* in September 2006 reported that the rate of ice melt on the vast island has tripled over the last several years. That same month a University of Colorado team published a study in *Nature* indicating that between April 2004 and April 2006 Greenland lost ice at a rate 2.5 times that of the preceding two years. In October 2006, a team of NASA scientists reported that the flow of glaciers into the sea was accelerating. Eric Rignot, a glaciologist at NASA's Jet Propulsion Laboratory, said, "None of this has been predicted by numerical models, and therefore all projections of the contribution of Greenland to sea level [rise] are way below reality."

At the other end of the earth, the 2-kilometer-thick Antarctic ice sheet, which covers a continent about twice the size of Australia and contains 70 percent of the world's fresh water, is also beginning to melt. Ice shelves that extend from the continent into the surrounding seas are starting to break up at an alarming pace.

In May 2007, a team of scientists from NASA and the University of Colorado reported satellite data showing widespread snow-melt on the interior of the Antarctic ice sheet over an area the size of California. This melting in 2005 was 900 kilometers inland, only about 500 kilometers from the South Pole. Konrad Steffen, one of the scientists involved, observed, "Antarctica has shown little to no warming in the recent past with the exception of the Antarctic Peninsula, but now large regions are showing the first signs of the impacts of warming."

The ice shelves surrounding Antarctica are formed by the flow of glaciers off the continent into the surrounding sea. This flow of ice, fed by the continuous formation of new ice on land and culminating in the breakup of the shelves on the outer fringe and the calving of icebergs, is not new. What is new is the pace of this process. When Larsen A, a huge ice shelf on the east coast of the Antarctic Peninsula, broke up in 1995, it was a signal that all was not well in the region. Then in 2000, a huge iceberg nearly the size of Connecticut—11,000 square kilometers, or 4,250 square miles—broke off the Ross Ice Shelf.

After Larsen A broke up, it was only a matter of time, given the rise in temperature in the region, before neighboring Larsen B would do the same. So when the northern part of the Larsen B ice shelf collapsed into the sea in March 2002, it was not a total surprise. At about the same time, a huge chunk of ice broke off the Thwaites Glacier. Covering 5,500 square kilometers, this iceberg was the size of Rhode Island.

The Pace of the Melting Accelerates

Even veteran ice watchers are amazed at how quickly the disintegration is occurring. "The speed of it is staggering," said Dr. David Vaughan, a glaciologist at the British Antarctic Survey, which has been monitoring the Larsen Ice Shelf closely. Along the Antarctic Peninsula, in the vicinity of the Larsen Ice Shelf, the average temperature has risen 2.5 degrees Celsius over the last five decades.

When ice shelves already largely in the water break off from the continental ice mass, this does not have much direct effect on sea level per se. But without the ice shelves to impede the flow of glacial ice, typically moving 400–900 meters a year, the flow of ice from the continent could accelerate, leading to a thinning of the ice sheet on the edges of the Antarctic continent. If this were to happen, sea level would rise accordingly.

The International Institute for Environment and Development (IIED) has analyzed the effect of a 10-meter rise in sea level, providing a sense of what the melting of the world's largest ice sheets could mean. The IIED study begins by pointing out that 634 million people live along coasts at or below 10 meters above sea level, in what they call the Low Elevation Coastal Zone. This massive vulnerable group includes one eighth of the world's urban population.

The Most Vulnerable Populations

One of the countries most vulnerable is China, with 144 million potential climate refugees. India and Bangladesh are next, with 63 and 62 million respectively. Viet Nam has 43 million vulnerable people, and Indonesia, 42 million. Others in the top 10 include Japan with 30 million, Egypt with 26 million, and the United States with 23 million.

The world has never seen such a massive potential displacement of people. Some of the refugees could simply retreat to higher ground within their own country. Others—facing extreme crowding in the interior regions of their homeland—would seek refuge elsewhere. Bangladesh, already one of the world's most densely populated countries, would face a far greater concentration: in effect, 62 million of its people would be forced to move in with the 97 million living on higher ground. Would a more sparsely populated country like the United States be willing to accommodate an influx of rising-sea refugees while it was attempting to relocate 23 million of its own citizens?

Not only would some of the world's largest cities, such as Shanghai, Kolkata, London, and New York, be partly or entirely inundated, but vast areas of productive farmland would also be lost. The rice-growing river deltas and floodplains of

Asia would be covered with salt water, depriving Asia of part of its food supply. This loss of prime farmland would parallel the loss of river water as Himalayan glaciers disappear.

Civilization's Downfall

In the end, the question is whether governments are strong enough to withstand the political and economic stress of relocating large numbers of people while suffering losses of housing and industrial facilities. The relocation is not only an internal matter, as a large share of the displaced people will want to move to other countries. Can governments withstand these stresses, or will more and more states fail? . . .

The risk facing humanity is that climate change could spiral out of control and it will no longer be possible to arrest trends such as ice melting and rising sea level. At this point, the future of civilization would be at risk.

This combination of melting glaciers, rising seas, and their effects on food security and low-lying coastal cities could overwhelm the capacity of governments to cope. Today it is largely weak states that begin to deteriorate under the pressures of mounting environmental stresses. But the changes just described could overwhelm even the strongest of states. Civilization itself could begin to unravel under these extreme stresses.

"Al Gore's claim that ocean levels will rise 20 feet thanks to global warming seems to ignore the laws of thermodynamics."

Global Warming Could Not Melt the Polar Ice Caps

Jerome J. Schmitt

Following the release of former Vice President Al Gore's documentary film An Inconvenient Truth, *some scientists began to question the validity of the film's claims regarding the imminent consequences of global warming. Jerome J. Schmitt, a mechanical engineer and the president of NanoEngineering Corporation, which researches and develops chemical technology for military and national defense purposes, is among those who have questioned the conclusions reached in the movie. Schmitt argues in the following viewpoint that the atmospheric temperature is not getting hotter nor is it causing significant melting of arctic glaciers. The author outlines the math used to back up his claims and contends that Gore's predictions of rising sea levels resulting from global warming are greatly exaggerated.*

Jerome J. Schmitt, "Will the Ice Caps Melt?" *American Thinker*, January 22, 2008. Reproduced by permission.

As you read, consider the following questions:

1. How many feet does Al Gore claim the ocean levels will rise as a result of global warming?

2. What example does the author use to show that temperature increases do not correlate with an immediate melting of snow and ice?

3. How much more heat does the author argue to be necessary over the next 100 years to melt arctic ice caps enough to raise sea levels?

There is considerable debate over whether the "greenhouse gas" effect will raise the temperature of the atmosphere by between 1–5°C over the next 100 years. But even if you grant for the sake of argument the Warmist claim that the earth's atmosphere will go up a full five degrees centigrade in temperature, [environmental activist and former vice president] Al Gore's claim that ocean levels will rise 20 feet thanks to global warming seems to ignore the laws of thermodynamics. I am no climatologist, but I do know about physics.

Global Warming Alarmists Overlook Facts

Anyone who has ever spent time in a temperate climate following a snowy winter realizes that when the air temperature rises above 32°F the snow and ice do not melt immediately. We may experience many balmy early spring days with temperatures well above freezing while snow drifts slowly melt over days or weeks. Similarly, lakes and ponds take some time to freeze even days or weeks after the air temperature has plunged below zero. This is due to the latent heat of freezing/melting of water, a physical concept long quantified in thermodynamics.

That aspect of basic physics seems to have been overlooked by climatologists in their alarming claims of dramatic and rapid sea-level rise due to melting of the Antarctic ice caps and Greenland glaciers. But of course, we have learned that models predicting global warming also failed to take account of precipitation, so overlooking important factors ("inconvenient truths") should not cause much surprise anymore.

The scientific data necessary to calculate the amount of heat necessary to melt enough ice to raise ocean levels 20 feet is readily available on the internet, and the calculations needed to see if polar cap melting passes the laugh test are surprisingly simple. Nothing beyond multiplication and division, and because we will use metric measures for simplicity's sake, much of the multiplying is by ten or a factor of ten.

Raising the Temperature of the Atmosphere

Let's review the math. The logic and calculations are within the grasp of anyone who cares to focus on the subject for [a] minute or two, and speak for themselves.

I should first mention that the only source of energy to heat the atmosphere is the sun. The average energy per unit time (power) in the form of sunlight impinging on the earth is roughly constant year-to-year, and there are no means to increase or reduce the energy flux to the earth. The question merely is how much of this energy is trapped in the atmosphere and available to melt ice thus effecting "climate change."

How much heat must be trapped to raise the atmospheric temperature by a degree centigrade (or more) can be readily calculated, knowing the mass of the atmosphere and the specific heat of air. Specific heat is simply an empirically-determined quantity that corresponds to the number of units of heat energy required to raise a specific mass of a substance, in this case air, by 1 degree in temperature. A common unit of energy familiar to most of us is the calorie. But for simplicity, in this calculation I will use the MKS [Meter, Kilogram, Second system of units] metric unit of the Joule (J), which, while

Global Warming Is Not Behind Tropical Storm Intensity

Increasing sea surface temperatures in the tropical Atlantic Ocean and measures of Atlantic hurricane activity have been reported to be strongly correlated since at least 1950, raising concerns that future greenhouse-gas-induced warming could lead to pronounced increases in hurricane activity. Models that explicitly simulate hurricanes are needed to study the influence of warming ocean temperatures on Atlantic hurricane activity, complementing empirical approaches. Our regional climate model of the Atlantic basin reproduces the observed rise in hurricane counts between 1980 and 2006, along with much of the interannual variability, when forced with observed sea surface temperatures and atmospheric conditions. Here we assess, in our model system, the changes in large-scale climate that are projected to occur by the end of the twenty-first century by an ensemble of global climate models, and find that Atlantic hurricane and tropical storm frequencies are reduced. At the same time, near-storm rainfall rates increase substantially. Our results do not support the notion of large increasing trends in either tropical storm or hurricane frequency driven by increases in atmospheric greenhouse-gas concentrations.

Thomas R. Knutson, Joseph J. Sirutis, Stephen T. Garner, Gabriel A. Vecchi, and Isaac M. Held, Nature, *May 18, 2008.*

perhaps unfamiliar to many readers in itself, is the numerator in the definition of our common unit of power, the Watt[†] = Joule/second.

The mass of the atmosphere [is approximately 5×10^{18} kg]. We also know that it is principally composed of air, so without loss of accuracy in what is essentially an "order of magnitude" calculation, it is fair to employ the specific heat of air at constant pressure, C_p. . . . While this has a value that changes with temperature, it doesn't change by orders of magnitude, consequently, I choose the value at 0° C, which, as we all know, is near to the global mean temperature at sea level. In this I err on the side of caution, overestimating the heat energy in the calculation below, because as we all know, both air pressure and temperature drop with altitude. Also note that while the specific heat value cited uses the unit °K in the denominator, this is equal to a °C. I use the tilde ($\sim$) as symbol for "circa" or "approximately."

Mass of atmosphere: 5 x 10^{18} kg

Specific heat of air: 1.005 kJ/kg-°C

Heat needed to raise the temp of the atmosphere 1° C: $\sim$5 x 10^{18} kJ

Heat needed to raise the temp of the atmosphere 5° C: **$\sim$2.5 x 10^{19} kJ**

Conditions Necessary to Raise Global Sea Levels

It is instructive now to compare this quantity of heat with the amount that would be required to melt sufficient volume of ice from the Antarctic ice to raise the sea-level by 20-feet as predicted by Al Gore. Although ice floats, ice and water are very close in density, so at first approximation, it is fair to say that the volume of sea-water required to raise sea-level by 20-feet would be equivalent to the volume of ice that would need to melt to fill the ocean basins in order to cause that rise. Consequently, let's first roughly calculate the volume of seawater necessary.

The surface area of the earth . . . is 5.1 x 10^8 square kilometers, which I convert to 5.1 x 10^{14} square meters below for the purpose of our calculation. Al Gore's 20-foot-rise is equal to ∼6 meters. Let's use the commonly cited figure that 70% of the earth's surface is covered by the oceans and seas. Accordingly,

Area of earth's surface: 5.1 x 10^{14} m^2

Proportion of earth's surface covered by water: 70%

Area of oceans and seas: ∼3.6 x 10^{14} m^2

Sea level rise predicted by Al Gore: 20 feet = 6 m

Volume of water necessary to raise sea-level 20-feet: ∼22 x 10^{15} m^3

Volume of ice that needs to melt to raise sea-level 20-feet: ∼22 x 10^{15} m^3

This is where the latent heat of melting comes into the equation. As we all know, when we drop an ice cube into our glass of water, soft-drink or adult beverage, it quickly cools the drink. Heat is transferred to the ice from the liquid in order to melt the ice; this loss of heat cools and reduces the temperature of the liquid. This cooling continues until the ice melts completely.

Scientists have long known that a mixture of ice and water (ice-water) remains at the freezing/melting point (0° C = 32°F). Adding heat does *not* change the temperature, it just melts more ice; withdrawing heat does *not* change the temperature, it just freezes more water. The temperature of ice-water will not rise until all the ice is melted; conversely, the temperature of ice-water will not fall until all the water is frozen. The heat that would have otherwise raised the ice temperature is somehow "stored" in the melt water—hence "latent heat." . . .

Reassessing Predictions of Sea Level Rise

It turns out that latent heats of melting (and evaporation) are generally very large quantities when compared to the amount of heat necessary to change temperatures. Also, as usual in such analyses we normalize to units of mass. Since the density of water/ice is roughly a thousand times higher than air, this also greatly impacts the magnitudes of energy involved, as you will see below. So let's proceed with the calculation.

The latent heat of melting of water . . . is 334 kJ/kg of water. One of the benefits of the metric system is that 1 ml = 1 cm^3 = 1 g of water; this "built in" conversion simplifies many engineering calculations. Remembering this fact, we do not need to look up the density of water. Converting this density, 1 g/cm^3, to MKS units, yields density of water = 1000 kg/m^3. We now have all our data for the rough calculation:

Volume of ice that needs to melt (from above): $\sim$22 x 10^{15}

Density of water and ice: 1000 kg/m^3

Mass of ice that needs to melt: $\sim$22 x 10^{18} kg

Latent heat of melting for water 3.34 x 10^2 kJ/kg

Heat necessary to melt ice to achieve 20-foot sea-level rise $\sim$ **7.4 x 10^{21} kJ**

Following this "back of the envelope" calculation, let's compare the two energy values:

Heat needed to raise the temp of the atmosphere 5° C: **$\sim$2.5 x 10^{19} kJ**

Heat necessary to melt ice to achieve 20-foot sea-level rise **$\sim$7.4 x 10^{21} kJ**

There is a difference of 30* between these two figures, by implication extending the time-horizon for sea-level rise from 100 to 3000 years at the earliest. This does *not* mean that ice caps have not melted in the distant past nor that ice-age glaciers have not grown to cover much of the northern hemisphere; it simply means that the time scales involved to move sufficient quantities of heat to effect such melting or freezing occur over what we scientists commonly call "geological" time scales, i.e. tens or hundreds of thousands of years.

Even if sufficient heat is trapped in the atmosphere to raise it the maximum value predicted by anthropogenic "glo-

---

* Editor's note: a transposed decimal point led to an incorrect multiple used here when this article was first published. The energy required is nevertheless hundreds of times greater than evidently assumed by Al Gore.

bal warming" alarmists (5° C) over the next 100 years, thirty times more heat energy must be imparted into the ice-caps to melt sufficient ice to raise sea-levels the catastrophic levels prophesied by Al Gore.

| "Projected impacts to polar bears from global warming will affect virtually every aspect of the species' existence."

Polar Bears Are Threatened by Global Warming

Kassie Siegel and Brendan Cummings

In the viewpoint that follows, Kassie Siegel and Brendan Cummings present scientific evidence to support their argument that global warming has created a situation in which the polar bear must be labeled a threatened species because the animal could become extinct within the next century. Specifically, they fear that, as a consequence of global warming, arctic sea ice is receding. Because of this, polar bears are unable to hunt as they have in the past, and thus the species' population is beginning to dwindle. The authors warn that if this loss of sea ice is not halted, polar bears will eventually lose the ability to reproduce due to malnutrition and reduced habitat. Kassie Siegel is the Senior Counsel and Climate Law Institute Director at the Center for Biological Diversity; Brendan Cummings is Senior Counsel and Oceans Director at the Center for Biological Diversity.

Kassie Siegel and Brendan Cummings, "Petition to List the Polar Bear (*Ursus maritimus*) as a Threatened Species under the Endangered Species Act," *Center for Biological Diversity*, February 16, 2005. Reproduced by permission.

As you read, consider the following questions:

1. What percentage of arctic, summer sea ice do the authors estimate will disappear by the end of the century?

2. Polar bear scientists predict that the polar bear population in the Western Hudson Bay in Canada may lose the ability to reproduce as early as what year?

3. List some of the examples given by the authors of the negative effects of global warming on polar bears.

The polar bear (*Ursus maritimus*) faces likely global extinction in the wild by the end of this century as [a] result of global warming. The species' sea-ice habitat is literally melting away. The federal Endangered Species Act (ESA) requires the protection of a species as "Threatened" if it "is likely to become an endangered species within the foreseeable future throughout all or a significant portion of its range." A species is considered an "endangered species" when it "is in danger of extinction throughout all or a significant portion of its range." Unfortunately, the endangerment of the polar bear and its likely extinction are all too foreseeable, as both polar bear and climate scientists agree that the species cannot survive the ongoing and projected loss of its sea-ice habitat in a warming Arctic. Absent substantial reductions in emissions of greenhouse gases, by century's end average annual temperatures in the Arctic will likely rise upwards of 7°C (13.6°F) and summer sea ice will decline by 50–100%. The polar bear cannot survive such changes and therefore meets the statutory criteria for protection as Threatened under the ESA. . . .

Scientists have been aware of global warming due to greenhouse gas emissions for over 30 years. That global warming is and will be more rapid and pronounced in the Arctic than in other areas of the world has been known and observed for nearly as long. Concern for the fate of the polar bear in a changing climate has been expressed for over a decade. However, in the past two years, with the release of the Arctic Climate Impact Assessment's (ACIA's) report on *Impacts of a Warming Arctic* (2004), combined with a peer-reviewed analysis by three of the world's foremost experts on polar bears, *Polar bears in a warming climate* (2004), that the polar bear faces a very real likelihood of extinction in the foreseeable future cannot be dismissed as mere speculation. Rather, the "best available science" demonstrates that global warming is occurring, that Arctic sea ice is melting, and that absent significant reductions in human-generated greenhouse gases, such continued warming and consequent reduction of sea ice will occur that the polar bear will face severe endangerment and likely extinction in the wild by the end of the century.

A Scientific Consensus on Global Warming

That global warming as a result of anthropogenic greenhouse gas emissions (primarily carbon dioxide, methane, and nitrous oxides) is occurring and accelerating is no longer subject to credible scientific dispute. In 2001 the Intergovernmental Panel on Climate Change (IPCC) released its *Third Assessment Report—Climate Change 2001*. The IPCC was established by the World Meteorological Organization and the United Nations Environment Programme in 1988. Its mission is to assess available scientific and socio-economic information on climate change and its impacts and the options for mitigating climate change and to provide, on request, scientific and technical advice to the Conference of the Parties to the United Nations Framework Convention on Climate Change. Since 1990, the IPCC has produced a series of reports, papers, methodologies, and other products that have become the standard works of reference on climate change. The *Third Assessment Report* is the product of over 2000 scientists from 100 countries participating in the most rigorously peer-reviewed scientific collaboration in history. In its *Summary for Policymakers*, the IPCC (2001) unequivocally stated that "[t]here is new and stronger evidence that most of the warming observed over the last 50 years is attributable to human activities." The IPCC further concluded that:

> Projections using the SRES [*Special Report on Emissions Scenarios*] emissions scenarios in a range of climate models result in an increase in globally averaged surface temperature of 1.4 to 5.8°C over the period 1990 to 2100. This is about two to ten times larger than the central value of observed warming over the 20th century and the projected rate of warming is very likely to be without precedent during at least the last 10,000 years, based on paleoclimate data.

In the four years since the 2001 IPCC Report, the scientific consensus on global warming has only grown stronger, and the warnings from climate scientists more urgent. While there is continuing scientific debate on specifics such as the rate or likely regional consequences of global warming, and while there are policy debates on what can and should be done to address global warming, the "best available science" clearly and unequivocally demonstrates that global warming is upon us and will bring profound changes to the world's climate over the course of this century and beyond.

The Impact of Global Warming in the Arctic

Global warming is already having pronounced impacts on the Arctic. In November 2004 the Arctic Climate Impact Assessment's report on *Impacts of a Warming Arctic* (2004) was released. The ACIA is "a comprehensively researched, fully referenced, and independently reviewed evaluation of arctic climate change and its impacts for the region and for the world. It has involved an international effort by hundreds of scientists over four years, and also includes the special knowledge of indigenous people." The ACIA report concludes that greenhouse gas driven climate changes "are being experienced particularly intensely in the Arctic. Arctic average temperature

The Polar Bear Is Listed as a Threatened Species

In many ways, the polar bear poses a unique conservation challenge. With most threatened and endangered species, we can identify a localized threat that we can seek to address. The threat to the polar bear, however, comes from global influences and their effect on sea ice.

While the legal standards under the ESA [Endangered Species Act] compel me to list the polar bear as threatened, I want to make clear that this listing will not stop global climate change or prevent any sea ice from melting. Any real solution requires action by all major economies for it to be effective. That's why I'm taking administrative and regulatory action to make certain the ESA isn't abused to make global warming policies.

Dick Kempthorne,
remarks at press conference on polar bear listing,
U.S. Department of the Interior, May 14, 2008.

has risen at almost twice the rate as the rest of the world in the past few decades. Widespread melting of glaciers and sea ice and rising permafrost temperatures present additional evidence of strong arctic warming." Significantly, "acceleration of these climatic trends is projected to occur during this century, due to ongoing increases in concentrations of greenhouse gases in the earth's atmosphere."

The ACIA's analysis and conclusions regarding Arctic temperature increases are dramatic. For example:

In Alaska and western Canada, winter temperatures have increased by as much as 3–4°C (5–7°F) in the past 50 years. Over the next 100 years, under a moderate emissions scenario, annual average temperatures are projected to rise

3–5°C (5–9°F) over land and up to 7°C (13°F) over the oceans. Winter temperatures are projected to rise by 4–7°C (5–9°F) over land and 7–10°C (13–18°F) over the oceans.

This ongoing and projected warming has already and will continue to severely reduce the extent of sea-ice coverage:

> Over the past 30 years, the annual average sea-ice extent has decreased by about 8%, or nearly one million square kilo-meters (386,100 square miles), an area larger than all of Norway, Sweden, and Denmark (or Texas and Arizona) combined, and the melting trend is accelerating. Sea-ice extent in summer has declined more dramatically than the annual average, with a loss of 15–20% of the late-summer ice coverage. Additional declines of 10–50% in annual average sea-ice extent are projected by 2100. Loss of sea-ice during summer is projected to be considerably greater, with a 5-model average projecting more than a 50% decline by late this century, and some models showing near-complete disappearance of summer sea ice.

In sum, the impacts of global warming on the Arctic are already being felt with a rise in temperature and a consequent decline in sea ice. Under relatively optimistic future emissions scenarios, summer sea ice will likely decline 50–100% by the end of the century. Under any scenario, the future of ice-dependent species such as the polar bear is grim.

The Consequences of Melting Sea Ice

Polar bears are completely dependent upon Arctic sea-ice habitat for survival. Polar bears need sea ice as a platform from which to hunt their primary prey (ringed seals, *Phoca hispida*), to make seasonal migrations between the sea ice and their terrestrial denning areas, and for other essential behaviors such as mating. Unfortunately, the polar bear's sea-ice habitat is quite literally melting away.

Canada's Western Hudson Bay population, at the southern edge of the species' range, is already showing the impacts of global warming. Break-up of the annual ice in Western Hudson Bay is now occurring on average 2.5 weeks earlier than it did 30 years ago. Earlier ice break-up is resulting in polar bears having less time on the ice to hunt seals. Polar bears must maximize the time they spend on the ice feeding before they come ashore, as they must live off built-up fat reserves for up to 8 months before ice conditions allow a return to hunting on the ice. The reduced hunting season has translated into thinner bears, lower female reproductive rates, and lower juvenile survival. While population declines are not yet evident in Hudson Bay, polar bear scientists calculate that if sea-ice trends continue, most female polar bears in the Western Hudson Bay population will be unable to reproduce by the end of the century, and possibly as early as 2012. Without reproduction, this population is doomed to extinction.

While Western Hudson Bay is the only population in which scientists have already observed negative impacts from climate change and published their results in peer-reviewed journals, impacts that have not yet been documented may be occurring in other less well-studied populations as well. Regardless, the consequences of future sea-ice reductions for polar bears globally will be severe. According to the ACIA, "the reduction in sea ice is very likely to have devastating consequences for polar bears, ice-dependent seals, and local people for whom these animals are a primary food source." The ACIA concludes that "polar bears are unlikely to survive as a species if there is an almost complete loss of summer sea-ice cover, which is projected to occur before the end of this century by some climate models. . . . The loss of polar bears is likely to have significant and rapid consequences for the ecosystems that they currently occupy."

A 2004 peer-reviewed analysis looking at all aspects of global warming's impacts on the polar bear by three of the world's foremost experts on the species, *Polar bears in a warming climate*, came to a similar conclusion as the ACIA, stating that "it is unlikely that polar bears will survive as a species if the sea ice disappears completely as has been predicted by some."

The Widespread Effect on Polar Bears

Even short of complete disappearance of sea ice, projected impacts to polar bears from global warming will affect virtually every aspect of the species' existence, in most cases leading to reduced body condition and consequently reduced reproduction or survival:

- The timing of ice formation and break-up will determine how long and how efficiently polar bears can hunt seals. A reduction in the hunting season caused by delayed ice formation and earlier break-up will mean reduced fat stores, reduced body condition, and therefore reduced survival and reproduction.

- Reductions in sea ice will in some areas result in increased distances between the ice edge and land. This will make it more difficult for female bears that den on land to reach their preferred denning areas. Bears will face the energetic trade-off of either leaving the sea ice earlier when it is closer to land or traveling farther to reach denning areas. In either case, the result is reduced fat stores and likely reduced survival and reproduction.

- Reductions in sea-ice thickness and concentration will likely increase the energetic costs of traveling as moving through fragmented sea ice and open water is more energy intensive than walking across consolidated sea ice.

- Reduced sea-ice extent will likely result in reductions in the availability of ice-dependent prey such as ringed seals, as prey numbers decrease or are concentrated on ice too far from land for polar bears to reach.

- Global warming will likely increase the rates of human/ bear interactions, as greater portions of the Arctic become more accessible to people and as polar bears are forced to spend more time on land waiting for ice formation. Increased human/bear interactions will almost certainly lead to increased polar bear mortality.

- The combined effects of these impacts of global warming on individual bear's reproduction and survival are likely to ultimately translate into impacts on polar bear populations. Impacts will be most severe on female reproductive rates and juvenile survival. In time, reduction in these key demographic factors will translate into population declines and extirpations.

In sum, changes in sea-ice extent, thickness, movement, fragmentation, location, duration, and timing will have significant and often adverse impacts on polar bear feeding, breeding, and movement. Such impacts will likely result in reduced reproductive success and higher juvenile mortality, and in some cases increased adult mortality. By century's end the combined effects of these demographic changes will likely result in population declines and extirpations, and possible global extinction of the species.

Immediate Action Must Be Taken

Summarizing the various likely impacts of global warming on the polar bear, [experts] come to the following sobering conclusion:

In contrast to many terrestrial and most marine species that may be able to shift northward as the climate warms, polar bears are constrained in that the very existence of their habitat is changing and there is limited scope for a northward shift in distribution. Due to the long generation time of polar bears and the current pace of climate warming, we believe it unlikely that polar bears will be able to respond in an evolutionary sense. Given the complexity of ecosystem dynamics, predictions are uncertain but we conclude that the future persistence of polar bears is tenuous.

In addition to the suite of impacts from global warming, polar bears also face additional threats such as increasing oil exploration and development and risk of oil spills throughout the Arctic, serious impacts to the immune system and reproductive system from exceptionally high levels of contaminants such as PCBs [an organic pollutant], unsustainable hunting and illegal poaching in some areas, and increased human activity in the Arctic. Global warming will likely interact with several of these additional threats in a synergistic and cumulative fashion, further increasing the polar bear's peril. . . .

The future of the polar bear is indeed grim. While most populations are currently reasonably healthy and the global population is not presently endangered, the species as a whole faces the likelihood of severe endangerment and possible extinction by the end of the century. As such, it will be endangered in the foreseeable future and therefore meets the criteria for listing now as Threatened under the ESA. While the polar bear will likely not disappear for several decades, decisions made and actions taken over the next decade will likely dictate whether the species can survive. Only with prompt action to drastically reduce greenhouse gas emissions can the future of the polar bear be assured. The United States must play a leading role in this global effort. Listing the species under the ESA is a small but significant step in that direction.

"What we do know about polar bears is that, contrary to media portrayals, they are not fragile 'canary in the coal mine' animals, but are robust creatures that have survived past periods of extensive deglaciation."

It Is Uncertain Whether Polar Bears Are Threatened by Global Warming

Kenneth P. Green

Images of endangered species of animals have long served as catalysts for environmental movements, spurring large groups of people to act quickly in order to protect a particular habitat or create wildlife reserves. Kenneth P. Green argues that environmentalists have most recently employed the polar bear and its supposed plight as a convenient tool to raise global awareness about the possible threats of global warming. Green contends that current methods of studying polar bear populations are insufficient in their findings to affirm conclusively that this animal's numbers are dwindling. Further, he states that even less evidence

Kenneth P. Green, "Is the Polar Bear Endangered, or Just Conveniently Charismatic?" *American Enterprise Institute Environmental Policy Outlook No. 2*, May 2, 2008. Reproduced with the permission of the American Enterprise Institute for Public Policy Research, Washington, D.C.

exists to imply a causal relationship between global warming and changes in polar bear populations. Kenneth P. Green is a resident scholar at the conservative public policy think tank, the American Enterprise Institute.

As you read, consider the following questions:

1. According to Green, which environmental groups use the polar bear's shrinking population as evidence that global warming is a serious problem?

2. What does the author believe to be possible consequences of placing the polar bear on the threatened species list?

3. Green gives three reasons why it is difficult to collect accurate data about polar bear populations; what are they?

Environmentalists have long used charismatic megafauna—large animals that invoke powerful attachments in humans—to raise awareness of and promote policy solutions to perceived environmental threats. Giant pandas, the symbol of the World Wide Fund for Nature, are a type of charismatic megafauna, as are "whales and other sea mammals, salmon and other inspirational fish, eagles and other flashy raptors." [as defined in the August 23, 1999 *Today* article, "Birth and Rebirth"] Other charismatic megafauna featured in environmental crusades include gorillas, grizzly bears, wolves, great white sharks, the Arctic lynx, African elephants, bighorn sheep, rhinoceroses, and, of course, penguins, which got a movie of their very own [*March of the Penguins*].

Such campaigns are highly effective. Environmental activist Eric de Place observes that using these types of animals as "poster children" [good examples] for broader conservation has worked with grizzly bears, wolves, and sea otters. And the money follows the glamour. Studies have shown that our spending preferences skew to the charismatic species: as economist Robert Stavins points out, the species we protect are generally "warm and cuddly."

The Poster Child for Arctic Conservation

The latest animal to become an environmental pet project is *Ursus maritimus,* the Latin name given to the polar bear. In the age of Knut—the polar bear cub orphaned by its mother and raised by humans in a German zoo—media coverage of polar bears has increased dramatically. And, of course, [former vice president and environmental activist] Al Gore featured the plight of the polar bear in his movie *An Inconvenient Truth.*

Polar bears are cute as cubs and majestic as adults. There are few animals with a higher "awwwwww" factor than a baby polar bear, and pictures of adult polar bears standing on icebergs in the far extremes of the Arctic cause an instinctual upwelling of respect for the powerful animals capable of surviving in an environment that humans can tread only with great preparation, and still at great risk. Virtually everyone wishes to ensure that polar bears are protected from excesses of human action that, as we have seen in the past, can indeed drive animal populations to extinction.

Environmental groups, claiming that man-made global warming threatens the polar bears' survival, have called for an endangered species listing that would have far-reaching consequences. Not only would such a listing place the Arctic region off limits for mineral exploration, but it would also open up still another line of attack for environmentalists trying to force emissions of greenhouse gases downward at all costs. Should the polar bear be listed as a threatened species, lawsuits to force companies and governments to reduce activities deemed harmful to the polar bear (emitting greenhouse gases) will be quick in coming.

Using the Polar Bear to Promote Regulation

Virtually every major environmental group trumpets the polar bears' peril. The Center for Biological Diversity tells us:

> Polar bears are at risk of extinction because global warming is causing catastrophic environmental change in the Arctic, including the rapid melting of sea ice. Because the bears are deeply dependent on the sea ice for their survival, they stand to become the first mammals in the world to lose 100 percent of their habitat to global warming.

The National Wildlife Federation, which sells cute little plush polar bears, warns us that "[p]olar bears are literally drowning from global warming, unable to swim the increasingly longer distances between land and receding sea ice." The Natural Resources Defense Council (NRDC) cautions:

> Polar bears are completely dependent on Arctic sea ice to survive, but 80 percent of that ice could be gone in 20 years and all of it by 2040. Polar bears are already suffering the effects: birth rates are falling, fewer cubs are surviving, and more bears are drowning.

The World Wildlife Fund warns that "[i]f current climate trends continue unabated, polar bears could become extinct by the end of this century." And Greenpeace tells us:

> Global warming is causing the Arctic ice pack to thin and melt at an unprecedented rate, and as it does, the polar bear is being pushed toward the brink of extinction. Polar bears live only in the Arctic, and they depend entirely on the pack ice—the frozen surface of the Arctic Ocean—as a platform to breed, raise their young, hunt and travel. Scientists are predicting an ice-free Arctic Ocean in summer by as early as 2050, which could quite possibly spell doom for this magnificent creature.

All of these environmental groups favor strong regulatory agendas to reduce greenhouse gases, and all have consistently opposed the use of Arctic regions for resource production. So it was perhaps inevitable that several environmental groups (the Center for Biological Diversity, Greenpeace, and NRDC) would petition the U.S. Fish and Wildlife Service to list the polar bear as a threatened species under the Endangered Species Act. As of this writing, the [George W.] Bush administration has not rendered a verdict on whether polar bears are to be placed on the endangered species list, but it seems likely that they will be. The legal deadline for doing so was January 9, 2007, a date that the administration missed, but it is claiming that the delay was procedural and not caused by a dispute about endangerment. Now a federal judge has given the administration a deadline of May 15, 2008, to make a final listing determination. [Polar bears were listed as "threatened" on May 15, 2008.]

Consequences of Labeling the Polar Bear a Threatened Species

Listing the polar bear as a threatened species would have significant public policy consequences. It would set a new precedent, representing the first linkage of species endangerment with global warming. Such a listing would basically wall off the entire Arctic region to exploration, resource extraction, and development—at least by U.S. companies—and a threatened species listing would give environmental groups the ability to sue future U.S. governments to force them to reverse climate change by whatever means necessary.

There is little doubt that such lawsuits would be filed quickly. According to the NRDC:

> Listing the polar bear guarantees federal agencies will be obligated to ensure that any action they authorize, fund, or carry out will not jeopardize the polar bears' continued existence or adversely modify their critical habitat, and the

U.S. Fish and Wildlife Service will be required to prepare a recovery plan for the polar bear, specifying measures necessary for its protection.

As [American author and astronomer] Carl Sagan observed, "Extraordinary claims require extraordinary evidence." This should be especially true when the stakes are significant and are likely to impose considerable costs or limitations on economic development. Walling off the Arctic and enabling environmental groups to sue greenhouse gas emitters in the name of polar bear protection would certainly impose high costs on future generations for whom environmentalists propose to preserve the polar bear.

So we must ask: is there "extraordinary evidence" that polar bears are threatened by man-made global warming sufficient to justify the remarkable claim of setting aside Arctic development and regulating the energy economy of the world for the sake of the animal? Truly understanding the state of the polar bear, and the best policy options for protecting this magnificent animal, requires answering three questions. First, what do we know about the health of polar bear populations? Second, what do we know about future threats to polar bears? And third, what is the best policy for protecting them?

Difficulties in Measuring Polar Bear Populations

Though they are highly photogenic creatures, polar bears are difficult to study for a variety of reasons. First, polar bears live in remarkably isolated and inhospitable parts of the Arctic. Second, polar bears are not stationary animals: they have a very large "home range"—the largest area that an animal normally visits during its lifetime—that often exceeds two hundred thousand square kilometers. . . . And third, the Arctic is such a hostile environment that one can conduct polar bear surveys only at certain times of year and in areas close to land masses. Survey results, therefore, may or may not be representative of the population as a whole. This makes establishing the health of existing polar bear populations—the very beginning of our inquiry—difficult.

Because they are not able to do a rigorous count of existing polar bears or accurately count the number of polar bear offspring over time, scientists must make population estimates based on limited data. Polar bears are counted by periodic flyovers of suspected polar bear habitat or by capturing and marking a subpopulation of bears, then using the frequency of recapture as a means to estimate the size of a population. Few subpopulations have been surveyed repeatedly, and the surveys that exist were taken over different years, some dating back to the 1980s. Where even these limited data are unavailable, population estimates are created basically from hearsay: local people report seeing a certain number of polar bears to researchers, who then estimate what size population would be needed to support such a number of sightings.

Given these uncertainties, the best estimate—guesstimate might be a better term—published by the International Union for Conservation of Nature (IUCN) Species Survival Commission's (SSC) Polar Bear Specialist Group, is that there are about twenty thousand to twenty-five thousand polar bears worldwide. The bears are spread out around the Arctic in nineteen separate subpopulations that researchers think are largely autonomous (noninterbreeding). The groups range in size from small groups of several hundred bears to a few larger groups of several thousand. . . .

Limitations in Assessing Threats to Polar Bears

Because scientists have limited population data for polar bear populations, and even less data on trends in these populations, claims about endangerment are essentially based on assumptions. The first assumption is that global warming has caused, and will cause, a predictable reduction in sea ice. The

Climate Change Scientists Must Gain Public Trust

Scientific honesty and clarity is vital to maintaining the independence and integrity of public policy. If the public lose trust in scientists then policy risks being set by vested interests. Over-stating the implications of preliminary research opens environmental science to damning critiques by the anti-environmental lobby. This could increase public cynicism and complacency about climate change and biodiversity loss; in much the same way that 'over-egging' intelligence reports on weapons of mass destruction has affected public attitudes concerning politicians' motives for the Iraq war.

Richard J. Ladle, Paul Jepson,
Miguel B. Araújo, Robert J. Whittaker,
Biodiversity Research Group, Oxford University, n.d.

second assumption holds that polar bear populations will dwindle because they are dependent on sea ice to hunt for prey. But each of these assumptions is fraught with problems.

As with most everything involving climate change, there is a paucity of good-quality, long-term data available. Prior to 1979, the extent of Arctic sea ice was measured haphazardly and sporadically. Some localized, nonstandardized measurements were taken periodically by ships without advanced positioning equipment and are not considered accurate. Satellite imaging has only allowed measurement from about 1979, coinciding with a period of climate warming, which makes it inherently nonrepresentative of longer time periods.

But from the limited data available, it does seem that in recent years the extent of Arctic sea ice has shown steady shrinkage. Overall, Northern Hemispheric ice cover has been trending downward at about 3 percent per decade. . . .

The Intergovernmental Panel on Climate Change (IPCC) summarizes Arctic ice changes in its most recent report:

> Satellite data indicate a continuation of the 2.7 ± 0.6% per decade decline in annual mean arctic sea ice extent since 1978. The decline for summer extent is larger than for winter, with the summer minimum declining at a rate of 7.4 ± 2.4% per decade since 1979. Other data indicate that the summer decline began around 1970.

It is that latter trend that is worrying with regard to polar bear population survival, as a significant number of polar bears use sea ice as a base for hunting, resting, and mating. . . .

The IPCC's computer modeling projects that Arctic ice decline will continue into the future. But the IPCC projections are based on the assumption that Arctic ice melting is the result of global warming caused by greenhouse gas emissions—an assumption that was recently shown to be of dubious merit by NASA, which is hardly a hotbed of climate skepticism.

In October 2007, NASA announced the results of an in-depth study of Arctic sea-ice melting and found that what has caused the unusually large melting seen in the last eight years was not greenhouse gas-induced global warming. In the press release describing the study, team leader Son Nghiem explained that the warming of recent years was, in fact, caused by a change in wind patterns. "Unusual atmospheric conditions set up wind patterns that compressed the sea ice, loaded it into the Transpolar Drift Stream and then sped its flow out of the Arctic," he said. When that sea ice reached lower latitudes, it rapidly melted in the warmer waters.

In January 2008, another study, published in the journal *Nature*, also cast doubt on whether greenhouse gas-induced heating is melting the Arctic. In a study looking at the vertical distribution of atmospheric heating, Nordic researchers found that, although models of greenhouse gas-induced warming predict that increased heat will show up close to the surface of the earth, the data show the opposite: Arctic heating has actually been happening too high in the atmosphere to reflect greenhouse gas causation. What the data seem to indicate is that heat from the tropics is being transported to the Arctic by wind patterns that are not well understood.

Thus, at present, we cannot assume the IPCC's future predictions for Arctic ice melt trends are meaningful. Recently observed Arctic melting could well be a shorter-term phenomenon unrelated to man-made global warming.

Incomplete Scientific Modeling

While data on polar bear populations are relatively scarce, data on population trends are nearly nonexistent. Thus, to determine whether polar bears will be endangered by the disappearance of sea ice, trends in population are predicted using something called population viability analysis (PVA), which is statistical modeling used to predict various outcomes within animal populations. The major meta-analysis of polar bear populations is the IUCN/SSC Polar Bear Specialist Group's 2005 report on the status of the polar bear. The report uses a type of stochastic subpopulation viability analysis, meaning that it incorporates random variability terms into PVA to come up with estimates of future sizes for polar bears by region. In the IUCN/SSC models, estimated polar bear mortality rates (from tag-and-recapture studies); litter sizes; sex ratio of cubs; initial subpopulation size; and the sex, age, and family status of killed polar bears are fed into a computer program that forecasts future population rates under a variety of input assumptions and random variation.

Like various statistical models, PVA can be a useful tool in policy cost-benefit analysis, but its results are only as accurate as the data and the model assumptions that go into it. Polar bear populations are difficult to measure, in part because they travel so much, are sparsely populated, and live far from people. The highest-quality data on polar bears come from aerial studies and mark/recapture studies, in which scientists "mark" polar bears and estimate how many are in a population based on sightings of marked and unmarked animals. There are other methods of estimating polar bears, but the report describes those methods as having "unknown and in most cases inestimable errors." Of the nineteen subpopulations of polar bears, the IUCN reports estimates based on aerial or mark/recapture data for fourteen, but of these, only five are based on data collected after 1998. Twelve had sufficient data for the report to predict population trends, and of the five marked as declining, only two of these estimates were based on aerial or mark/recapture data from after 1998. Scientists have collected more recent data on polar bear populations, but from studies with more "inestimable errors."

Even the highest-quality data available on polar bears may not be suitable for precise population predictions or extinction possibilities. The body of scientific literature on this subject shows the difficulties both of making predictions and of deriving confidence intervals. Also, PVA predictions for extinction or other outcomes over x number of years requires between 5x and 10x years of data. Unfortunately, although there are some mark/recapture data going back to the late 1960s and early 1970s for several subpopulations, there certainly are not enough data for anything close to precise estimates of polar bear populations over even the next ten years. There is simply too much uncertainty involved in modeling.

A Potentially High Error Rate

The IUCN report uses sedate statistical language to describe trends in polar bear populations and discusses causes other than climate change. For one of the subpopulations, it writes that the numbers "prohibit an unequivocal statistical conclusion that the sub-population has declined," but that based on observational evidence about polar bear health and data on neighboring groups of polar bears, the subpopulation is classified as declining. The report describes overharvesting by native populations and environmental pollutants, as well as warming temperatures and earlier ice breakup, as possibly negatively affecting various subpopulations.

There are some broader criticisms of polar bear population forecasts that J. Scott Armstrong, Kesten C. Green, and Willie Soon make in "Polar Bear Population Forecasts: A Public-Policy Forecasting Audit." Armstrong, a professor at the Wharton School [college of business at the University of Pennsylvania], has led a movement to codify forecasting procedures and is sharply critical of predictions that fail to live up to these standards, especially when they are invoked in calls for large-scale public policy changes. The types of criticisms that Armstrong et al. make of government reports arguing that polar bears should be listed as a threatened species relate to data, methodology, assessing uncertainty, data presentation and feedback, and independence and heterogeneity of authors. Last year [2007], the U.S. Geological Survey released nine papers on the status of polar bears to inform the U.S. Fish and Wildlife Service in their decision about whether to add polar bears to the endangered species list. By their standards, the two reports Armstrong and his colleagues examined—"Forecasting the Rangewide Status of Polar Bears at Selected Times in the 21st Century" and "Polar Bears in the Southern Beaufort Sea II: Demography and Population Growth in Relation to Sea Ice Conditions"—properly apply only 10 percent and 15 percent of the forecasting principles, respectively.

Even with an adequate data set, it is possible that a PVA can still have large errors in extinction rate predictions. It is impossible to incorporate all future possibilities into a PVA: habitats may change, catastrophes may occur, and new diseases may be introduced. PVA utility can be enhanced by multiple model runs with varying sets of assumptions, including the forecast future date. Thoughts about the utility of PVA are mixed among scientists: PVA may be more useful when it is used to evaluate relative rather than absolute risks to populations under different policies.

Polar Bears Are Not a Fragile Species

At present, polar bear populations are robust and, according to native people, are considerably larger than they were in previous decades. Predictions of polar bear endangerment are based on two sets of computer models: one set predicts how much Arctic sea ice will melt as a result of global warming, and the other predicts how polar bear populations will respond. But computer models of climate are known to be fraught with problems, and the ecological models used to predict polar bear response are equally limited.

Because of extreme limitations in data, it is essentially impossible to decide whether polar bears are endangered and whether their habitat is threatened by man-made global warming or other natural climate cycles. This is acknowledged by the experts themselves—the actual IUCN/SSC report is more broad in naming causes and more conservative about estimating their effects.

What we do know about polar bears is that, contrary to media portrayals, they are not fragile "canary in the coal mine" animals, but are robust creatures that have survived past periods of extensive deglaciation. Polar bear fossils have been dated to over one hundred thousand years, which means that polar bears have already survived an interglacial period when temperatures were considerably warmer than they are at present and when, quite probably, levels of summertime Arctic sea ice were correspondingly low.

In discussions of whether to drill in the Arctic, one of the arguments raised by environmentalists is that this would harm the habitats of the many creatures, including polar bears, that make their homes in Alaska. If polar bears are placed on the endangered species list, the legal hurdles to oil and gas drilling will increase. There are two subpopulations of polar bears in Alaska. One of them, the Southern Beaufort Sea population, is shared with Canada, and the other, the Chukchi Sea population, with Russia. Best estimates for these areas show approximately 3,500 polar bears total in these two subpopulations. Last year, Shell Offshore Inc. was about to start drilling in the Beaufort Sea area when a court order halted the activity on the grounds that the federal government did not thoroughly assess the environmental impact before granting permission to drill.

In petitioning against the drilling, environmental groups invoked sea ducks, whales, and, of course, polar bears, as well as the effect that drilling could have on native populations. The U.S. Minerals Management Service estimates that the area holds the potential for 7 billion barrels of recoverable oil and 32 trillion cubic feet of recoverable natural gas. With oil at over $100 a barrel and natural gas at $7.60 per one thousand cubic feet, these are some very expensive polar bears.

"WHO [World Health Organization] now says that 150,000 deaths annually are attributable to the effects of climate change."

Global Warming Will Negatively Impact Human Health

Daniel J. Weiss and Robin Pam

Daniel J. Weiss and Robin Pam believe that the environmental changes occurring as a result of global warming are well-publicized but worry that most people ignore the possibly devastating impact global warming could have on humans worldwide. Weiss and Pam argue in the following viewpoint that climate change could potentially cause human populations around the world to experience increased rates of death and disease as well as the destruction of food supplies and shelter. The authors call on the U.S. government to take immediate action to halt what they see as the impending destruction faced by communities in both the United States and abroad. Daniel J. Weiss is a Senior Fellow and Director of Climate Strategy at the Center for American Progress, a progressive, public policy institute; Robin Pam is an assistant editor at the Center for American Progress.

Daniel J. Weiss and Robin Pam, "The Human Side of Global Warming," Center for American Progress, April 10, 2008. This material was created by the Center for American Progress, www.americanprogress.org.

As you read, consider the following questions:

1. The World Health Organization associates which vector-borne diseases with climate change, and how many deaths do these diseases bring annually?

2. According to the authors, in what ways could climate change result in increased hunger worldwide?

3. What two examples of climate change-related phenomena do the authors believe capable of displacing millions of people from their homes?

By now, global warming has been linked to melting glaciers and ice caps, higher average temperatures, and prolonged drought. What's not as well-known are the non-headline grabbing effects that the warming climate will have on human health. . . .

Several major public health organizations are calling attention to the devastating toll that climate change will take on the health of our children, families, and communities the world over. The Senate Committee on Health, Education, Labor, and Pensions [held a hearing April 10, 2008] on the public health challenges of climate change. The World Health Organization [WHO] has declared the theme of [the 2008] annual World Health Day "protecting health from climate change." And [2008's] National Public Health Week is themed "Climate Change: Our Health in the Balance."

In a hearing on the subject . . . in front of the House Select Committee on Energy Independence and Global Warming, chaired by Rep. Ed Markey (D-MA), Howard Frumkin, director of the Centers for Disease Control's National Center for Environmental Health, testified, "The science is clear that carbon dioxide does contribute to climate change . . . and as I have testified here today, climate change presents public health challenges."

Global Warming Linked to Severe Health Risks

Some of the most severe health effects linked to global warming include the following:

More illness and death resulting from heat waves. Increased frequency and severity of heat waves will lead to more heat stroke and other heat-related illness and death. Senior citizens and children are particularly vulnerable to these effects. The world has already seen the effects of heat on human health: The summer 2003 heat wave in Europe that claimed 35,000 lives was likely made worse by global warming, and in the summer of 2007, Greece suffered a massive heat wave and record wildfires. Eleven of the past 12 years rank among the hottest on record, and the Centers for Disease Control reports that heat waves already account for more deaths annually in the United States than hurricanes, tornadoes, floods, and earthquakes combined. The death toll is projected to increase as heat waves become more frequent.

Worsening air pollution causes more respiratory and cardiovascular disease. Air pollution worsens as temperatures increase, and higher levels of ozone smog and other pollutants have been directly linked with increased rates of respiratory and cardiovascular disease, including asthma and cardiac disarryhthmia. Pediatric asthma has already increased over the past 25 years, and global warming will only exacerbate children's suffering. Global warming is projected to most heavily affect the level of ground-level ozone in U.S. cities in the Northeast, Midwest, and West.

Vector-borne disease infections will rise. Currently, malaria, diarrhea, malnutrition, and floods related to climate change cause about 150,000 worldwide deaths annually, according to the World Health Organization. The range of malaria-carrying mosquitoes is spreading, too, to cooler places that have never before seen the disease, such as South Korea and the highlands of Papua New Guinea.

157

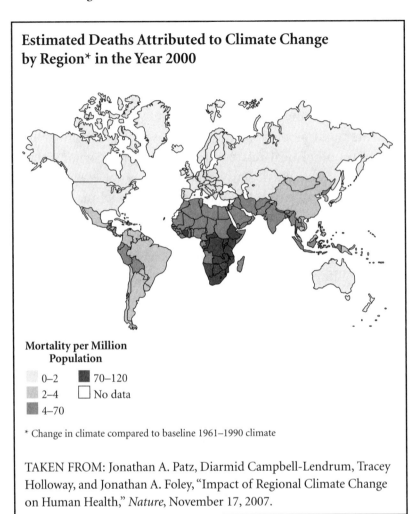

Estimated Deaths Attributed to Climate Change
by Region* in the Year 2000

**Mortality per Million
Population**

0–2   70–120
2–4   No data
4–70

* Change in climate compared to baseline 1961–1990 climate

TAKEN FROM: Jonathan A. Patz, Diarmid Campbell-Lendrum, Tracey
Holloway, and Jonathan A. Foley, "Impact of Regional Climate Change
on Human Health," *Nature*, November 17, 2007.

With warming temperatures, the breeding cycle of malaria-
carrying mosquitoes is shortening, which means more mosquitoes—and malaria—each year. The same effects will likely
be seen with other vector-borne diseases, such as Dengue fever, which infected 60,000 people in one outbreak in Brazil's
Rio de Janeiro [in 2008]. In the United States, viruses such as
West Nile, Hantavirus, and Lyme disease could increase their
ranges or spread more quickly with changing weather, and
formerly prevalent malaria or Dengue fever could re-emerge.

Weather-Related Health Effects

Changing food production and security may cause hunger. Rising temperatures and varying rainfall patterns could affect staple crop production and food security, while aiding the migration and breeding of pests that can devastate crops. Farmers in the tropical developing world will likely see decreases in production. Such changes could be devastating to people in poor countries, even while some cold climate nations, such as Canada, may expand their arable land.

With the prices of wheat, rice, and other staples already rising rapidly, the developing world can ill afford any production decreases at home. In addition, more severe weather, such as monsoons or hurricanes, can destroy crops and leave entire communities without food. And if hunger wasn't bad enough already, the Intergovernmental Panel on Climate Change recently concluded that up to 250 million more Africans could be left without potable [drinkable] water due to climate-related stresses within the decade.

More severe and frequent wildfires will threaten more people. Severe heat can also increase the frequency and intensity of wildfires, which threaten homes, lives, and livelihoods, and cause poor air quality. Autumn [2007] wildfires in California that displaced more than 1 million people were linked to the record southern California drought. And those were only the beginning. The Nobel Prize-winning Intergovernmental Panel on Climate Change has determined that "a warming climate encourages wildfires through a longer summer period that dries fuels, promoting easier ignition and faster spread . . . North America very likely will continue to suffer serious loss of life and property."

Flooding linked to rising sea levels will displace millions. Rising sea levels make coastal areas more susceptible to storm surges and flooding that result from severe weather. The most susceptible areas are densely populated river deltas and coastal cities in Asia—the Ganges River Delta, the Mekong River

Delta, islands in the Indian Ocean and South Pacific. [In 2007], almost 7 million people were displaced by flooding in Dhaka, Bangladesh, and in 2004, floods there killed more than 700. With displacement comes increased transmission of water-borne disease from stagnant water, the challenge of feeding and sheltering the displaced, sewage backups and squalid conditions, and strained disaster relief resources.

Combating Global Warming Will Save Lives

In the 1990s, more than 600,000 deaths occurred worldwide as a result of weather-related disasters. WHO now says that 150,000 deaths annually are attributable to the effects of climate change. Further, as Congresswoman Hilda L. Solis noted at the House Select Committee hearing on global warming and public health, these effects "will disproportionately affect the sick, poor, elderly, and communities of color." Solis urged her "colleagues to recognize the relationship between our climate and health and to work toward achieving climate justice." ... Solis and Markey introduced a resolution in the House, and Sen. Bernie Sanders (I-VT) a similar one in the Senate, that calls attention to the public health effects of global warming.

These human effects are real and immediate, but they can also be lessened if the United States takes the lead in transitioning to a low-carbon economy and reducing our greenhouse gas emissions now.

While the [George W.] Bush administration has tried to suppress information regarding the human health consequences of its lax approach to climate change, a 2004 EPA [Environmental Protection Agency] internal memo affirmed that "climate change has global consequences for human health and the environment." ... There is still a lack of decisive action in the United States. ... But the signs are clear. We can't afford to wait any longer.

*"For Britain, it is estimated a 3.6°F in-
crease will mean 2,000 more heat
deaths but 20,000 fewer cold deaths."*

Global Warming Will Lead to Fewer Human Deaths

Bjorn Lomborg

*Danish economist Bjorn Lomborg argues in the following view-
point that global warming will reduce the number of climate-
related deaths each year. Lomborg points out that while 35,000
deaths throughout Europe due to the 2003 heat wave is significant, it is important to note that approximately 25,000 people
die in England and Wales each winter. The author argues that
while increases in temperature worldwide due to global warming
will inevitably cause heat-related deaths, the climate change will
prevent nearly ten times as many deaths that would have been
caused by extreme cold.*

As you read, consider the following questions:

1. What did the Earth Policy Institute predict would be the
   result of the 2003 heat wave deaths?

Bjorn Lomborg, "Global Warming, the Great Lifesaver," *Discover*, August 31, 2007. Reproduced by permission.

2. According to the author, how many people die as a result of excess heat in Europe annually, and how many die from excess cold?

3. The author states that death rates in Philadelphia and across the United States have changed in what way and for what reason since the 1960s?

The heat wave in Europe in early August 2003 was a catastrophe of heartbreaking proportions. With more than 3,500 dead in Paris alone, France suffered nearly 15,000 fatalities from the heat wave. Another 7,000 died in Germany, 8,000 in Spain and Italy, and 2,000 in the United Kingdom: The total death toll ran to more than 35,000. Understandably, this event has become a psychologically powerful metaphor for the frightening vision of a warmer future and our immediate need to prevent it.

The green group Earth Policy Institute, which first totaled the deaths, tells us that as "awareness of the scale of this tragedy spreads, it is likely to generate pressure to reduce carbon emissions. For many of the millions who suffered through these record heat waves and the relatives of the tens of thousands who died, cutting carbon emissions is becoming a pressing personal issue."

All Deaths Should Be Weighted Equally

While 35,000 dead is a terrifyingly large number, all deaths should in principle be treated with equal concern. Yet this is not happening. When 2,000 people died from heat in the United Kingdom, it produced a public outcry that is still heard. However, the BBC recently ran a very quiet story telling us that deaths caused by cold weather in England and Wales for the past years have hovered around 25,000 each winter, casually adding that the winters of 1998–2000 saw about 47,000

High CO$_2$ Concentrations Enhance Human Health

Although historical and projected future increases in the air's CO$_2$ [carbon dioxide] concentration and its wrongly-predicted ability to lead to catastrophic global warming have been universally hailed by climate alarmists as diabolically detrimental to human health, scientific studies clearly demonstrate that such is not the case. Throughout the entire course of the Industrial Revolution, during which time the air's CO$_2$ content rose by 35% and its near-surface temperature by about 0.6°C, there has been no detectable negative impact on human longevity. In fact, human lifespan has concurrently experienced an almost unbelievable increase that shows no signs of ultimately leveling off or even slowing down. What is more, warming has been shown to *positively* impact human health, while atmospheric CO$_2$ enrichment has been shown to *enhance* the health-promoting properties of the food we eat, as well as stimulate the production of more of it. . . .

In light of these many well-documented observations, it is abundantly clear we have nothing to fear from increasing concentrations of atmospheric CO$_2$ and global warming, . . .

Source: Sherwood B. Idso, Craig D. Idso, and Keith E. Idso,
Enhanced or Impaired?: Human Health in a CO$_2$-Enriched
Warmer World, *Center for the Study of Carbon Dioxide
and Global Change, November 2003.*

cold deaths each year. The story then goes on to discuss how the government should make the cost of winter fuel economically bearable and how the majority of deaths are caused by strokes and heart attacks.

It is remarkable that a single heat-death episode of 35,000 from many countries can get everyone up in arms, whereas cold deaths of 25,000 to 50,000 a year in just a single country pass almost unnoticed. Of course, we want to help avoid another 2,000 dying from heat in the United Kingdom. But presumably we also want to avoid many more dying from cold.

For Europe as a whole, about 200,000 people die from excess heat each year. However, about 1.5 million Europeans die annually from excess cold. That is more than seven times the total number of heat deaths. Just in the past decade, Europe has lost about 15 million people to the cold, more than 400 times the iconic heat deaths from 2003. That we so easily neglect these deaths and so easily embrace those caused by global warming tells us of a breakdown in our sense of proportion.

Humans Will Adapt to Changing Temperatures

How will heat and cold deaths change over the coming century with global warming? Let us for the moment assume— very unrealistically—that we will not adapt at all to the future heat. Still, the biggest cross-European cold/heat study concludes that for an increase of 3.6 degrees Fahrenheit in the average European temperatures, "our data suggest that any increases in mortality due to increased temperatures would be outweighed by much larger short-term declines in cold-related mortalities." For Britain, it is estimated a 3.6°F increase will mean 2,000 more heat deaths but 20,000 fewer cold deaths. Likewise, another paper incorporating all studies on this issue and applying them to a broad variety of settings in both developed and developing countries found that "global warming may cause a decrease in mortality rates, especially of cardiovascular diseases."

But of course, it seems very unrealistic and conservative to assume that we will not adapt to rising temperatures throughout the 21st century. Several recent studies have looked at adaptation in up to 28 of the biggest cities in the United States. Take Philadelphia. The optimal temperature seems to be about 80°F. In the 1960s, on days when it got significantly hotter than that (about 100°F), the death rate increased sharply. Likewise, when the temperature dropped below freezing, deaths increased sharply.

Yet something great happened in the decades following. Death rates in Philadelphia and around the country dropped in general because of better health care. But crucially, temperatures of 100°F today cause almost no excess deaths. However, people still die more because of cold weather. One of the main reasons for the lower heat susceptibility is most likely increased access to air-conditioning. Studies seem to indicate that over time and with sufficient resources, we actually learn to adapt to higher temperatures. Consequently we will experience fewer heat deaths even when temperatures rise.

Periodical Bibliography

The following articles have been selected to supplement the diverse views presented in this chapter.

Peter Curson   "Climate Change and Human Health," *Geodate,* August 2007.

Erika Engelhaupt   "Global Warming Increases Deadly Air Pollution," *Environmental Science & Technology,* March 1, 2008.

Future Survey   "Climate Change as a Security Risk," October 2008.

Jim Giles   "Climate Change to Stunt Developing Nations' Growth," *New Scientist,* January 17, 2009.

Barbara Juncosa   "Suffocating Seas," *Scientific American,* October 2008.

Marc Kaufmanthe   "Climate Change Causes Warmest Year in 2006," *Christian Science Monitor,* January 11, 2007.

William Laurance   "Comment: Move Over, Polar Bear," *New Scientist,* January 10, 2009.

Joseph Mayton   "Egyptian Officials, Farmers Debate Effect of Climate Change on Fertile Nile Delta," *Washington Report on Middle East Affairs,* January/February 2009.

Aria Pearson   "The Perfect Storm," *New Scientist,* January 3, 2009.

Sid Perkins   "Portrait of a Meltdown," *Science News,* December 22, 2007.

John Roskam   "Did Global Warming Send Lehman Brothers Broke?" *Institute of Public Affairs Review,* November 2008.

OPPOSING
VIEWPOINTS®
SERIES

CHAPTER 4

How Can Global Warming Be Mitigated?

Chapter Preface

Several anti–global warming Web sites enumerate the steps individuals can take to reduce carbon emissions and curb their impact on climate change. Almost all of the organizations sponsoring these sites suggest the following: Replace incandescent light bulbs with compact fluorescent light bulbs (CFLs), inflate car tires to proper levels, replace or clean air filters on vehicles and furnaces, set home thermostats down by two degrees in the winter and up in the summer, purchase fuel efficient or hybrid cars, weatherproof homes, and turn off unused televisions and other electronic devices. Some of these Web sites even encourage consumers to change their shopping habits. They recommend buying locally grown food to save on transportation fuel used to truck foods to supermarkets. They also suggest purchasing goods that have less packaging to save on waste. At least one site advocates eating less meat to reduce the demand for cattle, which are significant producers of methane, a greenhouse gas.

Skeptics of this push to "go green" argue that many of the measures are impractical and costly. The *Daily Mail*, a newspaper in the United Kingdom, posted an editorial online that found fault with the European movement to ban incandescent lighting in favor of the energy-saving fluorescent alternative. The editors stipulate that the new CFLs are more expensive and produce a harsher light that needs time to warm up to the right intensity. "Because they must be kept on so much longer to run efficiently, the actual amount of energy saved by these bulbs has been vastly exaggerated," the *Daily Mail* asserts. "In addition to this, low-energy bulbs are much more complex to make than standard bulbs, requiring up to ten times as much energy to manufacture. Unlike standard bulbs, they use toxic materials, including mercury vapour, which the EU [European Union] itself last year banned from landfill sites—which means that recycling the bulbs will itself create an enormously expensive problem."

Most of these critics also claim that the cost and responsibility of global warming is being foisted on the public when corporate office buildings are routinely left lit up at night and industry remains a prime contributor of greenhouse gases. Ann Widdecombe, a commentator for another U.K. news journal, contends, "As usual, it is the ordinary citizen who will be persecuted—and almost certainly eventually prosecuted—while the big energy wasters carry on wasting." Widdecombe and others further point out that switching light bulbs and making other household adjustments is simply inconsequential given that the industries and power plants of nations such as China, India, and the United States are producing the lion's share of greenhouse emissions.

Lester Brown, the president of the Earth Policy Institute, an environmental think tank, however, takes issue with such skepticism. In his view, embracing low-energy light bulbs and making common appliances energy efficient would mean that the world could do away with more than 1,400 coal plants. In the following chapter, other environmental spokespersons proffer large-scale agendas for curbing the impact of global warming. Arrayed against these optimists are critics who foresee limitations or problems associated with adopting such measures as viable ways to reduce dependence on fossil fuels and cut greenhouse gas emissions.

> *"The most efficient way to apply a car-
> bon tax is at a relatively small number
> of major carbon bottlenecks, which
> cover the lion's share of [greenhouse
> gases]."*

A Carbon Tax Will Help Curb Global Warming

Ralph Nader and Toby Heaps

*In the following viewpoint, Ralph Nader and Toby Heaps advo-
cate instituting a flat carbon tax on major carbon dioxide producers across the globe. Nader and Heaps insist that this tax
would be more equitable than a cap-and-trade system, which the
authors believe could be undermined by poor management and
the ability of heavy polluters to relocate their industries to regions that had not reached their "cap," or limit, on carbon emissions. According to Nader and Heaps, a flat carbon tax would
compel polluting industries to retool, and the revenues raised
could be used to invest in environmentally conscious activities—
like saving rainforests—that would further decrease the impact*

Ralph Nader and Toby Heaps, "We Need a Global Carbon Tax," *Wall Street Journal*, vol.
252, December 3, 2008, p. A17. Copyright © 2008 Dow Jones & Company, Inc. All
rights reserved. Reprinted with permission of The Wall Street Journal

of carbon emissions. Nader is a consumer advocate and three-time presidential candidate. Heaps is the coordinator of Option 13, a campaign that works toward establishing a successor to the Kyoto Protocol.

As you read, consider the following questions:

1. As Nader and Heaps report, how much money does the Intergovernmental Panel on Climate Change estimate it will cost per year to thwart the progress of global warming?

2. By what year do the authors suggest an effective global tax should have stabilized atmospheric concentrations of greenhouse gases?

3. What is the "carrot" that the authors state could entice nations in the developing world to phase in a carbon tax?

If President Barack Obama wants to stop the descent toward dangerous global climate change, and avoid the trade anarchy that current approaches to this problem will invite, he should take [former vice president and environmental] Al Gore's proposal for a carbon tax and make it global. A tax on CO_2 emissions—not a cap-and-trade system—offers the best prospect of meaningfully engaging China and the U.S., while avoiding the prospect of unhinged environmental protectionism.

China emphatically opposes a hard emissions cap on its economy. Yet China must be part of any climate deal or within 25 years, notes Fatih Birol, chief economist at the International Energy Agency, its emissions of CO_2 could amount to twice the combined emissions of the world's richest nations, including the United States, Japan and members of the European Union.

According to the world authority on the subject, the Intergovernmental Panel on Climate Change (IPCC), it will cost

$1.375 trillion per year to beat back climate change and keep global temperature increases to less than two degrees Celsius (3.6 degrees Fahrenheit).

Heading Toward Trade Anarchy

Cap-and-traders assume, without much justification, that one country can put a price on carbon emissions while another doesn't without affecting trade or investment decisions. This is a bad assumption, given false comfort by the Montreal Protocol treaty, which took this approach to successfully rein in ozone-depleting gases. Chlorofluorocarbons are not pervasive like greenhouse gases (GHGs); nor was the economy of 1987 hyperglobalized like ours today.

Good intentions to limit big polluters in some countries but not others will turn any meaningful cap into Swiss cheese. It can be avoided by relocating existing and new production of various kinds of CO_2-emitting industries to jurisdictions with no or virtually no limits. This is known as carbon leakage, and it leads to trade anarchy.

How? The most advanced piece of climate legislation at the moment, the Lieberman-Warner Climate Security Act, contains provisions for retaliatory action to be taken against imports from carbon free-riding nations. Married with the current economic malaise, the temptation to slide into a righteous but runaway environmental protectionism—which Washington's K Street lobbyists would be only too happy to grease—would almost certainly lead to a collapse of the multilateral trading system. This scenario was presented to the world's trade ministers [in] December [2007] at the United Nations climate talks in Bali by David Runnalls of the International Institute for Sustainable Development.

True, trade anarchy might reduce emissions via a massive global depression. But there would be a lot of collateral damage. Because of the sheer scale of the challenge and the state

Offsetting the Tax Burden

[The] natural aversion to carbon taxes can be overcome if the revenue from the tax is used to reduce other taxes. By itself, a carbon tax would raise the tax burden on anyone who drives a car or uses electricity produced with fossil fuels, which means just about everybody. Some might fear this would be particularly hard on the poor and middle class.

But Gilbert Metcalf, a professor of economics at Tufts, has shown how revenue from a carbon tax could be used to reduce payroll taxes in a way that would leave the distribution of total tax burden approximately unchanged.

N. Gregory Mankiw,
"One Answer to Global Warming: A New TAX,"
New York Times, *September 16, 2007.*

of the hyperglobalized economy, we will need the same price on carbon everywhere, or it won't work anywhere.

The Elements of an Efficient and Equitable Tax

President Obama can define his legacy in the first 100 days [of his presidency] by laying the groundwork for a global tax on carbon dioxide emissions that is effective, efficient, equitable and enforceable. An effective, harmonized tax on CO_2 emissions must stabilize the growth of atmospheric concentrations of GHGs by no later than 2020. The tax must also be adjusted annually, by a global body, according to this objective.

The IPCC has crunched the numbers and says this means a tax of about $50 levied on every metric ton of GHGs, or carbon dioxide equivalent (CO_2e to use their terminology). In the short-term, consumers would feel the pinch. But the tax would pave the way for cheaper, cleaner energy and ways of getting around.

The most efficient way to apply a carbon tax is at a relatively small number of major carbon bottlenecks, which cover the lion's share of GHGs. The key points where flows of carbon are the most concentrated include: trunk pipelines for gas, refineries for oil, railroad heads for coal, liquid natural gas (LNG) terminals, cement, steel, aluminum and GHG-intensive chemical plants.

Collecting and spending the bulk of revenues from a carbon tax must remain the sovereign right of participating nations. For instance, nations could decide to make the tax revenue-neutral by reducing taxes on income or helping finance industrial retooling for a green economy.

However, we in the rich world must recognize our culpability for creating three-quarters of this global warming mess, as well as our greater capacity to finance industrial retooling. Thus, there could be a carrot for developing-world nations which commit to applying the phased-in carbon tax: Access to a portion of the carbon tax levies from rich countries to help preserve forests and to prepare for climate change through flood walls, improved irrigation, drought resistant crops, desalination facilities, and the like. This is no small change: 10% of $50/metric ton CO_2e carbon tax levied in all rich countries would be $100 billion per year. The stick for carbon free-riding countries would come in the form of incrementally severe penalties, leading up to countervailing duties on carbon-intensive imports.

Monitoring Large Pollution Sources

A global carbon tax levied on a relatively small number of large sources can be monitored by satellite and checked against the annual surveillance of fiscal and economic polices already carried out by IMF [International Monetary Fund] staff. Thus, the accounting involved is much more precise and much less subject to the vagaries of corruption and conflict over which industries and companies get their free handouts of carbon credits—carbon pork—than in a cap-and-trade system.

There are three reasons why countries, such as China and India, that have traditionally resisted any notion of a common responsibility to make current polluters pay would do well to enlist in this effort.

First, while there is no limit on the downside for missing a hard cap, with a carbon tax you just pay as you go. If a fast-growing country like China accepted an emissions cap and then overshot it, they would have to purchase carbon credits on the international market. If they missed their target by a lot, carbon credits would be scarce, and purchasing them would suck dry their foreign exchange reserves in one slurp. That's why a carbon tax is much easier to swallow and, anyway, through the power of the price signal, it would produce the same desired result as a hard cap.

Second, administering billions of dollars of carbon credits in a cap-and-trade system in an already chaotic regulatory environment would invite a civil war between interest groups seeking billions in carbon credit handouts and the regulator holding the kitty. By contrast, a uniform tax on CO_2 emissions levied at a small number of large sites would be relatively clear-cut. During the Montreal Protocol talks in the 1980s, India smartly balked at a suggestion to phase out CFCs [dangerous particles commonly found in aerosols] in certain products and not in others because of the chaos that would result from the ambiguity.

Third, key people in China read our newspapers. They see the ominous clouds of protectionism under the guise of environmentalism in bills like Lieberman-Warner and they don't want to be harmed; neither should we, given the trillions of dollars of Treasury bills they hold. Showing compliance with a harmonized carbon tax at a small number of large bottleneck points would be child's play compared to the chaos of cap-and-trade.

If President Obama hits the ground running fast in the direction of a global carbon tax, he can usher in a new dawn that might finally make peace between man and climate.

"Over the past two decades, tradable permit systems for pollution control have been adopted with increasing frequency in the United States as well as other parts of the world."

A Cap-and-Trade Program Will Help Curb Global Warming

Robert N. Stavins

Robert N. Stavins is a professor of business and government and is the director of the Harvard University Environmental Economics Program. In the following viewpoint, Stavins maintains that the problem of carbon dioxide pollution can be effectively limited by instituting a global cap-and-trade program, one that sets a "cap" on the amount of carbon emissions a group of polluters can produce and then allows those who pollute less than the cap to trade emissions credits to those who cannot keep their pollution levels under the cap. In Stavins' view, because the cap is incrementally lowered every few years, polluters will be forced to adopt more carbon controls over time or pay out more and

Robert N. Stavins, "A U.S. Cap-and-Trade System to Address Global Climate Change," *Hamilton Project*, October 2007. Reproduced by permission.

more money to purchase emissions credits. Stavins contends that such a program will work for carbon emissions because similar systems have already shown success in curbing other types of pollutants.

As you read, consider the following questions:

1. What does Stavins mean when he contends that a carbon emissions cap should be imposed "upstream"?

2. In what two ways does Stavins say carbon emissions credits may be distributed to industries?

3. What does the author say has been previously the most important application in the United States of a market-based instrument for environmental protection?

There is general consensus among economists and policy analysts that a market-based policy instrument targeting CO_2 emissions—and potentially some non-CO_2 greenhouse gas emissions—should be a central element of any domestic climate policy. Two alternative market-based instruments—a cap-and-trade system and a carbon tax—have been advocated. Although there are trade-offs between them, this [viewpoint] will argue that the better approach and the one more likely to be adopted in the short to medium term in the United States is a cap-and-trade system.

The environmental effectiveness of a domestic cap-and-trade system for climate change can be maximized and its costs and risks minimized by inclusion of several specific features. The system should target all fossil fuel-related CO_2 emissions through an economy-wide cap on those emissions. The cap should be imposed "upstream," that is, on fossil fuels at the point of extraction, processing, or distribution, not at the point of combustion. The system should set a trajectory of caps over time that begin modestly and gradually become more stringent, establishing a long-run price signal to encourage investment in emission-reducing technology. It should adopt mechanisms to protect against cost uncertainty. And it should include linkages with the climate policy actions of other countries. Importantly, by providing politicians with the option to mitigate economic impacts through the distribution of emissions allowances, this approach can establish consensus for a policy that achieves meaningful reductions. It is for these reasons and others that cap-and-trade systems have been used increasingly in the United States to address an array of environmental problems, for example to phase out the use of lead in gasoline, limit emissions of sulfur dioxide (SO_2) and nitrous oxides (NO_x), and phase out chlorofluorocarbons (CFCs). . . .

How Cap-and-Trade Works

A cap-and-trade system places a cap, or ceiling, on the aggregate emissions of a group of regulated sources by creating a limited number of tradable emissions allowances for a given period and requiring firms to surrender a quantity of allowances equal to their emissions during that period. The system imposes no particular limits on emissions from any given firm or source. A firm may emit as much as it chooses, as long as it obtains sufficient allowances to do so. The government may initially distribute the allowances for free or sell them at auction. In either case, the need to surrender valuable allowances to cover any emissions and the opportunity to trade those allowances establishes a price on emissions. In turn, this price provides firms with an incentive to reduce their emissions that influences all of their production and investment decisions.

Because allowances are tradable, the ultimate distribution of emissions reduction efforts necessary to keep emissions within the cap is determined by market forces. Those sources that find it cheaper to reduce their emissions than to continue emitting and pay for allowances will do so, and those that find it cheaper to purchase allowances will do so. Through the trading of allowances, the price adjusts until emissions are

"Cap and Trade" Is Essential

Our environmental goal and economic objectives can best be accomplished through an economy-wide, market-driven approach that includes a cap and trade program that places specified limits on GHG [greenhouse gas] emissions. This approach will ensure emission reduction targets will be met while simultaneously generating a price signal resulting in market incentives that stimulate investment and innovation in the technologies that will be necessary to achieve our environmental goal. The U.S. climate protection program should create a domestic market that will establish a uniform price for GHG emissions for all sectors and should promote the creation of a global market.

United States Climate Action Partnership,
"A Call for Action," 2007. www.us-cap.org

brought down to the level of the cap. Firms' ability to trade emissions allowances creates a market in which allowances migrate toward their highest-valued use, covering those emissions that are the most costly to reduce. A well-designed cap-and-trade system thus minimizes the costs of achieving any given emissions target. Overall, a cap-and-trade system provides certainty regarding emissions from the regulated sources as a group, because *aggregate* emissions from all regulated entities cannot exceed the total number of allowances.

The cost of achieving significant greenhouse gas emissions reductions in future years will depend critically on the availability and cost of low- or nonemitting technologies. A cap-and-trade system that establishes caps extending decades into the future generates price signals that provide incentives for firms to invest in the development and deployment of such technologies, thereby lowering the future cost of reducing emissions. To create these incentives, a cap-and-trade system must provide credible commitments to meeting long-run emissions targets. If a lack of credibility makes the payoff from investments in the new technologies highly uncertain, these investments will lag. On the other hand, policymakers also need to maintain flexibility to adjust long-term targets as new information is obtained regarding the benefits and costs of mitigating climate change. Managing this trade-off between the credibility of long-run targets and flexibility is important for the success of any climate policy. . . .

Previous Cap-and-Trade Successes

Over the past two decades, tradable permit systems for pollution control have been adopted with increasing frequency in the United States as well as other parts of the world. . . .

The first important example of an environmental trading program in the United States was the phasedown of leaded gasoline in the 1980s. Although not strictly a cap-and-trade system, the phasedown included features, such as trading and banking of environmental credits, that brought it closer than other credit programs to the cap-and-trade model and resulted in significant cost savings. The program was successful in meeting its environmental targets, and the system was cost-effective, with estimated cost savings of about $250 million a year. Also, the program provided measurable incentives for the diffusion of cost-saving technology.

A cap-and-trade system was also used in the United States to help comply with the Montreal Protocol, an international agreement aimed at slowing the rate of stratospheric ozone depletion. The protocol called for reductions in the use of CFCs [particles commonly found in aerosols that are dangerous contributors the greenhouse effect] and halons, the primary chemical groups thought to lead to depletion. The timetable for the phaseout of CFCs was later accelerated, and the system appears to have been relatively cost-effective.

The most important application in the United States to date of a market-based instrument for environmental protection is arguably the cap-and-trade system that regulates SO_2 emissions, the primary precursor of acid rain. The program, established under the U.S. Clean Air Act Amendments of 1990, is intended to reduce SO_2 and NO_x emissions by 10 million tons and 2 million tons, respectively, from 1980 levels. A robust market in SO_2 allowances emerged under the program, resulting in cost savings on the order of $1 billion annually compared with some command-and-control alternatives. The program has also had a significant environmental impact: SO_2 emissions from the electric power sector decreased from 15.7 million tons in 1990 to 10.2 million tons in 2005.

"Nuclear power is the only mature, major source of electric power in the United States that is essentially carbon-free."

Nuclear Energy Should Be Part of the Solution to Curb Global Warming

Matt Bennett, Rob Keast, and John Dyson

Matt Bennett, Rob Keast, and John Dyson are members of Third Way, a Washington, D.C.-based think tank advocating progressive political change. Bennett is the vice president for public affairs, Keast is a senior policy advisor, and Dyson is a trustee for the organization. In the viewpoint that follows, the three authors claim that to address global warming in the short term, America should embrace carbon-free nuclear power. Although the authors acknowledge that other alternative energy sources—such as wind and solar power—are valuable contributors to a carbon-free agenda, only nuclear energy, they say, has the capacity to meet America's energy needs in the immediate future. For this reason, Bennett, Keast, and Dyson assert that politicians and the public need to be better informed about the advantages of nuclear power.

Matt Bennett, Rob Keast, and John Dyson, "Another Inconvenient Truth: Solving Global Warming and Energy Security Requires Nuclear Power," *Third Way*, April 23, 2007. Reproduced by permission.

As you read, consider the following questions:

1. According to the authors, what quantity of carbon emissions was prevented by the nuclear generating capacity of the United States in 2005?

2. What percentage of America's total electricity output do the authors say that nuclear power is expected to contribute in the year 2030?

3. Why do the authors believe that advocates of renewable energies have undercut the seriousness of their own arguments by ignoring nuclear energy?

It's on the cover of news magazines and has become a daily staple in newspapers. It's brought pictures of swimming polar bears, melting glaciers, and grassy Alpine ski slopes. It's helped garner an Academy Award and a Nobel Prize nomination for [environmentalist and former vice president] Al Gore.

Climate change is, well, hot. It is widely discussed, and not just at the policy level—it's become water-cooler talk and Oprah fodder. It has even made its way into a [George W.] Bush State of the Union address, albeit for less than a sentence and for the first time ever in 2007. And a *Drudge Report* headline screams "Tomorrow's Forecast: Chaos" in response to a major new scientific report on climate change.

We count ourselves among the convinced. Climate change could be among the greatest existential threats that humanity has ever known.

To address this pressing problem, there are a range of options available to policymakers and the public, including reliance on alternative fuels and conserving energy use to mandating controls on carbon emissions. Many of these ideas are worthy of strong support or at least serious consideration. This is a huge, many-sided problem, and it requires a broad, multifaceted set of solutions.

However, few in the environmental community or their allies in policymaking have championed—indeed, most have actively opposed—the one climate change solution that can make a substantial difference in the near term: nuclear power. This raises a serious problem—there does not seem to be a realistic path to resolving climate change that does not significantly expand nuclear energy, but most of those at the frontlines of fighting climate change have not yet embraced it. We must resolve this contradiction if we are to confront global warming effectively. . . .

The Need to Expand Nuclear Power

The facts are quite simple, and they speak for themselves: nuclear power is the only mature, major source of electric power in the United States that is essentially carbon-free. In 2005, nuclear power made up 19 percent of our energy mix and prevented 3.32 million tons of sulfur dioxide, 1.05 million tons of nitrogen oxide and *681.9 million tons of carbon dioxide* emissions in the United States alone.

But that is today. US electricity demand is predicted to rise by 45% by 2030. That means 350,000 megawatts of new generation capacity must be built to meet that demand. Unless this country changes course, coal will constitute a larger share of new power generation than it would otherwise.

One reason is that growth of domestic nuclear power production had, until very recently, totally stalled. There are currently 103 licensed reactors in the US, at 65 plant sites in 31 states. Most have gotten or will get 20-year license extensions from the Nuclear Regulatory Commission (NRC). But no new nuclear power plants have been brought online since 1996, and since 1973, every new plant order—totaling more than 100—has been cancelled. Moreover, industry consolidation has meant that fewer firms are operating nuclear plants.

There is some good news of late—the 2005 Energy Policy Act provides various incentives which support currently operating plants and encourages future construction. Since the 2005 law was passed, 13 companies have filed licenses with the NRC to build as many as 31 new reactors.

But the growth in nuclear production is not without controversy—serious debates relating to nuclear waste and plant safety continue. Still, we think the risks are worth taking. America has grappled with a nuclear waste dilemma for decades—it is a serious and currently unsolved problem, but we believe it can be managed safely in the short term and handled effectively in the long term.

America Must Take the Risk

As for plant safety, there is simply no such thing as completely risk-free power, and nuclear is no exception. That being said, our nuclear sites are some of the most fortified, well-protected industrial spaces in the nation. The industry's security is regulated and closely watched by on-site federal inspectors and overseers, and the FBI has categorized nuclear plants as "difficult targets." Furthermore, a new generation of plant design and technologies has made nuclear facilities more efficient, safe and less costly than in the past.

Yet despite good safety records and a recent resurgence in interest in new reactors, on its current trajectory, total nuclear generation is projected to grow from 780 billion kilowatt-hours in 2005 to only 896 billion kilowatt-hours in 2030 (that is, if the new reactors cited above come on-line). Even with this projected increase, the nuclear share of total electricity generation is expected to *fall* from 19 percent in 2005 to 15 percent in 2030. We would need another four plants (for a total of 35 new plants) simply to maintain nuclear power's current piece of the US energy pie.

So from a global warming perspective, the American energy production outlook is not great now, and, without substantial change, it is projected to get much worse. . . .

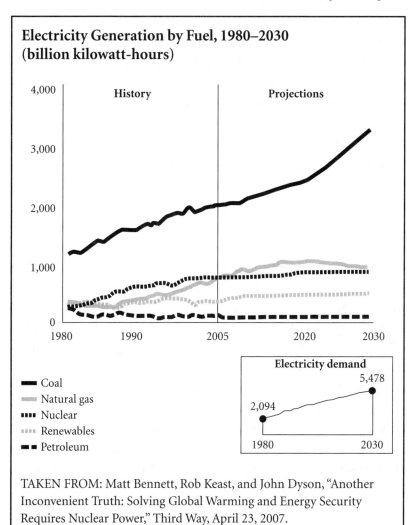

Electricity Generation by Fuel, 1980–2030 (billion kilowatt-hours)

- Coal
- Natural gas
- Nuclear
- Renewables
- Petroleum

Electricity demand
2,094 — 5,478
1980 — 2030

TAKEN FROM: Matt Bennett, Rob Keast, and John Dyson, "Another Inconvenient Truth: Solving Global Warming and Energy Security Requires Nuclear Power," Third Way, April 23, 2007.

That, in our view, is an unacceptable outcome. We must face the reality that a growing population and evolving technology will place ever-increasing demands on our energy production. We believe that policymakers and advocates should set as a general goal that we expand non- or low-carbon sources, such as nuclear, wind, solar, and "clean coal," to meet much of the new demand for power that our expanding nation and modern life require. As a specific and measurable target, we should aim to advance nuclear energy to a point where it provides for 25 percent of America's energy. This is an ambitious but achievable goal; unless we get closer to it, meeting increased energy needs while dealing with the reality of climate change is probably a pipe-dream.

Americans' Opinions Fluctuate

Recent public opinion polling reveals a seeming paradox: Americans believe that global warming is real, but they don't feel any urgency about dealing with it.

A Pew poll in January [2007] found that 77% of Americans believe there is solid evidence of global warming, and the same number believe global warming is a very serious or somewhat serious problem. But another Pew poll [in 2006] of global attitudes found that only 19% of Americans who had heard of global warming expressed a great deal of personal concern over the issue, the smallest percentage of any country in a survey of 15 nations. And climate change ranks 20th out of 23 in Pew's annual list of policy priorities (only 38% rank it as a top priority). Another January [2007] poll found that less than half of respondents said global warming worries them "a great deal" or "a good amount." In short, awareness of climate change is high, but urgency—and demand for government action—is low.

In part, this is because the solutions that many offer seem incommensurate to the scope of the problem. For example, almost no one disagrees that we should use more solar power, but solar makes up 1/30th of 1 percent of current US power usage. It is a very important but very small part of a near- or even mid-term solution. We simply must have more mature, low-carbon power generation methods if we are to address this issue aggressively over the next several decades.

One glaring problem is the failure on the part of leading climate change advocates—from most environmental groups to leading Members of Congress—to support the only existing, mature energy source that can almost immediately help save our planet from catastrophic climate change. . . .

Despite what some are calling a "nuclear renaissance" that is pegged to the climate issue and rising power needs, anti-nuclear forces have worked hard to muddy the waters. For example, the following polling question was asked on a survey by the Civil Society Institute:

> Experts have proposed a range of long-term and short-term solutions to the energy crisis and the threat posed by global warming. Some solutions—including solar energy and wind power—are already in place and would be expanded in the near-term. Others—such as increased conservation—could start immediately. Still others—including nuclear power and hydrogen fuel cells—would take a decade to put in place, or longer. What is your view of the best way for America to proceed? . . . [T]he energy and global warming problem is happening now. [Would you say] we need most of the emphasis placed on immediate and near-term solutions that will deliver fast results or we need most of the emphasis placed on solutions that will deliver results a decade from now or later?

Not surprisingly, 62% of respondents to this sharply slanted and misleading question said we need to take action now. Never mind that solar and wind are not mature power generation techniques and simply *cannot* provide "near term solutions" to our CO_2 problems.

Many advocates have taken this approach, attempting to keep the debate fixed solely on conservation and renewable sources. And no one denies that both are crucial to addressing the problem of global warming—a solution is impossible without real shifts in public behavior and a huge increase in our investment in renewable energy.

But we believe that by talking only about conservation and renewable energy, advocates have undercut the seriousness of their own argument on climate change. The American public may not know much about base-load capacity, but they understand that we are not going to get out of our CO_2 problem by relying solely on wind farms or geothermal power at this point in time. And they may be reluctant to make hard changes in their own lives—or demand policy fixes to climate change—until environmentalists start making some tough choices too. . . .

Nuclear Power Can Be More Efficient

One important reason that nuclear power production stalled in the 1990s involved the extraordinary inefficiencies built into the system. Every new plant was required to have its own unique design, leaving this nation with a patchwork of different reactors, using different parts and procedures. This massively drove up costs of construction and made operation and maintenance much more expensive and difficult, because parts were not interchangeable and personnel had to learn a new plant every time they went there. By contrast, countries like France, which draws 78 percent of its power from nuclear energy, built essentially the same two plants throughout the country.

Thankfully, the United States seems to have learned a lesson from that experience, and it now seems standardized reactor design will be the way of the future for domestic production of nuclear power plants. This will not only reduce the costs of construction, operation and maintenance, it will improve training, efficiency and, ultimately, safety. Furthermore, many new reactors will be built where plants already exist, further increasing efficiencies and reducing start-up and construction costs.

Other efficiencies were built into the 2005 Energy Policy Act, which is helping to fuel some resurgence of nuclear power development in the US. Still, more needs to be done. Both to deepen the impact that nuclear power itself can have on US emissions and to demonstrate to the public that we can make real progress on climate change, policymakers must ensure that new nuclear power plants can be constructed safely, affordably and efficiently. . . .

A Call to Action

On March 9, 2007, at a meeting of European Union heads of state, leaders made a commitment to reducing greenhouse gas emissions to 20% below 1990 levels, and stated explicitly that nuclear would be a part of the mix as a non-carbon source of energy. It is time for leaders in the United States to speak that plainly, both in making a commitment to reducing emissions overall and in embracing nuclear as a significant part of that effort. With "earth in the balance," as Al Gore once wrote in his visionary book of the same name, strong action and hard choices are required of everyone, and this is one that we believe progressive leaders of all stripes must take.

| "The case against nuclear power as a global warming remedy begins with the fact that nuclear-generated electricity is very expensive."

Nuclear Energy Should Not Be Part of the Solution to Curb Global Warming

Mark Hertsgaard

In the following viewpoint, independent journalist and author Mark Hertsgaard notes that nuclear power is often touted as a cheap and carbon-free energy that should be expanded to meet the threat of global warming. However, Hertsgaard argues that once the price of building nuclear reactors is factored into the equation, nuclear power is the most expensive form of energy. He further points out that because nuclear energy has been harnessed only to provide electricity, it would have little effect on the heating of buildings or the operating of vehicles—the two main contributors of global carbon emissions. For these reasons, Hertsgaard claims that America must look elsewhere for a remedy to carbon pollution.

Mark Hertsgaard, "Nuclear Energy Can't Solve Global Warming," *San Francisco Chronicle*, August 7, 2005, B1. Reproduced by permission of the author.

As you read, consider the following questions:

1. According to Hertsgaard, on what do environmentalists base their objections to nuclear power?

2. How does the author use his "Rolls-Royce" analogy to point out the expense of nuclear energy?

3. What does Hertsgaard claim would be a cheaper and quicker remedy to global warming than embracing nuclear power?

During a public lecture in San Francisco [in July 2005], Jared Diamond, the mega-selling author of *Guns, Germs and Steel*, became the latest and most prominent environmental intellectual to endorse nuclear power as a necessary response to global warming.

Addressing an overflow crowd at the Cowell Theater about why some societies fail and others don't (the theme of his most recent book, *Collapse*), Diamond three times cited global warming as a threat that could ruin modern civilization. During the question period, he was asked if he agreed with Stewart Brand, whose Long Now Foundation was sponsoring the lecture, that global warming posed such a grave threat that humanity had to embrace nuclear power.

It was a delicate moment, because Brand, the former editor of the *Whole Earth Catalogue*, was on stage with Diamond.

"I did not know that Stewart Brand said that," Diamond replied. "But yes, to deal with our energy problems we need everything available to us, including nuclear power." Nuclear, he added, should simply be "done carefully, like they do in France, where there have been no accidents."

"I did not expect that answer," Brand said.

Neither, it seemed, did much of the audience. Overwhelmingly white and affluent, they had nodded reverentially at everything Diamond said—about the self-destructiveness of ancient civilizations that leveled forests (Easter Island) or eroded soils (the Mayans) in pursuit of short-term gain, about the need for America to rethink its "core value" of consumerism if it hopes to survive. They had applauded when Diamond mocked President [George W.] Bush's see-no-evil approach to environmental protection. Yet here was Diamond urging an expansion of nuclear power, a technology most environmentalists regard as irredeemably evil.

A Seemingly Obvious Solution

"Deal with it," crowed Brand as the crowd sat in stunned silence. It was smug but useful advice, for this debate is bound to intensify. The Bush administration and much of Congress are pushing hard to revive the nuclear industry, which provides 20 percent of America's electricity but has not had a new reactor order since 1974.

In June [2005], Bush became the first president in 26 years to visit a nuclear power plant, the Calvert Cliffs facility near Washington, D.C., where he endorsed nuclear as an "environmentally friendly" energy source. His administration's 2006 budget increased nuclear power funding by 5 percent, even as it cut overall energy funding.

Congress followed suit in its recent energy bill. Besides giving the nuclear industry $7 billion in research-and-development subsidies and $7.3 billion in tax breaks, the bill contains unlimited taxpayer-backed loan guarantees and insurance protection for new reactors.

Diamond may not agree with Bush about much, but their shared support for nuclear power hints at the other factor that will drive the future debate. As the United States experiences more killer heat waves and out-of season hurricanes like this summer's, more Americans will recognize what the rest of the world has long accepted: Global warming is here, it will get worse, and the costs will be enormous. As we cast about for alternatives to the carbon-based fuels that are cooking our planet, nuclear power seems to be an obvious answer.

As Vice President Dick Cheney observed in 2001 when defending the administration's energy plan, which urged constructing hundreds of new nuclear plants, fission produces no greenhouse gases.

Risk Is Not the Issue

But the truth is that nuclear power is a weakling in combatting global warming. Investing in a nuclear revival would make our global warming predicament worse, not better. The reasons have little to do with nuclear safety, which may be why environmentalists tend to overlook them.

Environmentalists center their critique on safety concerns: Nuclear reactors can suffer meltdowns from malfunctions or terrorist attacks; radioactivity is released in all phases of the nuclear production cycle from uranium mining through fission; the problem of waste disposal still hasn't been solved; civilian nuclear programs can spur weapons proliferation. But absent a Chernobyl-scale disaster, such arguments may not prove to be decisive.

In an atmosphere of desperation over how to keep our TVs, computers and refrigerators humming in a globally warmed world, economic considerations will dominate. This is especially so when dissident greens like Diamond and Brand say nuclear safety is a solvable problem. Diamond is correct that France has generated most of its electricity from nuclear power for decades without a major mishap.

Dissident greens concede there are risks to nuclear power. But those risks, they say, are less than the alternatives. Coal, the world's major electricity source, kills thousands of people a year right now through air pollution and mining accidents. Coal is also the main driver of climate change, which is on track to kill millions of people in the 21st century—not in the sudden bang of radioactive explosions but the gradual whimper of environmental collapse as soaring temperatures and ris-

Nuclear Power Is Not Cost-Effective

Nuclear power is the slowest and costliest way to reduce CO_2 emissions, as financing nuclear power diverts scarce resources from investments in renewable energy and energy efficiency. The enormous costs of nuclear power per unit of reduced carbon emissions would actually worsen our ability to abate climate change as we would buy less carbon-free energy per dollar spent on nuclear power compared to emissions we would save by investing those dollars in solar, wind or energy efficiency. According to a Massachusetts Institute of Technology study on the future of nuclear power, 1,500 new nuclear reactors would have to be constructed worldwide by mid-century for nuclear power to have a modest impact on the reduction of greenhouse gasses.

Alice Slater, Pacific Ecologist, *Winter 2008.*

ing seas submerge cities, parch farmlands, crash ecosystems and spread disease and chaos worldwide.

Fear of such an apocalypse led the British scientist James Lovelock to become the first prominent environmentalist to endorse nuclear power as a global warming remedy, in 2003. Patrick Moore, a co-founder of Greenpeace (who left the group [in the mid-1990s]), soon echoed Lovelock's apostasy, as did Hugh Montefiore, a board member of Friends of the Earth, UK. All three were criticized by fellow greens. Likewise in the United States, the movement's major organizations remain adamantly anti-nuclear. But environmentalists on both sides of this argument are overlooking the strongest objection to nuclear power, even as the nuclear industry hopes no one notices it. The objection is rooted in energy economics, hence the oversight.

Nuclear Energy Is Expensive

As energy economist Joseph Romm argued in a blog exchange with Brand, "It is too often the case that experts on the environment think they know a lot about energy, but they don't."

The case against nuclear power as a global warming remedy begins with the fact that nuclear-generated electricity is very expensive. Despite more than $150 billion in federal subsides over the past 60 years (roughly 30 times more than solar, wind and other renewable energy sources have received), nuclear power costs substantially more than electricity made from wind, coal, oil or natural gas. This is mainly due to the cost of borrowing money for the decade or more it usually takes to get a nuclear plant up and running.

Remarkably, this inconvenient fact does not deter industry officials from boasting that nuclear is the cheapest power available. Their trick is to count only the cost of operating the plants, not of constructing them. By that logic, a Rolls-Royce is cheap to drive because the gasoline but not the sticker price matters. The marketplace, however, sees through such blarney. As Amory Lovins, the soft energy guru who directs the Rocky Mountain Institute, a Colorado think tank that advises corporations and governments on energy use, points out. "Nowhere (in the world) do market-driven utilities buy, or private investors finance, new nuclear plants." Only large government intervention keeps the nuclear option alive.

Nuclear Power Addresses Only a Small Part of Global Warming

A second strike against nuclear is that it produces only electricity, but electricity amounts to only one third of America's total energy use (and less of the world's). Nuclear power thus addresses only a small fraction of the global warming problem, and has no effect whatsoever on two of the largest sources of carbon emissions: driving vehicles and heating buildings.

The upshot is that nuclear power is seven times less cost-effective at displacing carbon than the cheapest, fastest alternative—energy efficiency, according to studies by the Rocky Mountain Institute. For example, a nuclear power plant typically costs at least $2 billion. If that $2 billion were instead spent to insulate drafty buildings, purchase hybrid cars or install super-efficient lightbulbs and clothes dryers, it would make unnecessary seven times more carbon consumption than the nuclear power plant would. In short, energy efficiency offers a much bigger bang for the buck. In a world of limited capital, investing in nuclear power would divert money away from better responses to global warming, thus slowing the world's withdrawal from carbon fuels at a time when speed is essential.

Mainstream environmentalists do argue that energy efficiency, solar, wind and other renewable fuels are better weapons against global warming than nuclear is. But they will fare better if they go a step further and point out that embracing nuclear is not just unnecessary but a step backward.

Even so, a tough fight lies ahead. As the energy bill illustrates, the nuclear industry has many friends in high places. And the case for nuclear power will strengthen if its economics improve. The key to lower nuclear costs is to reduce construction times, which could happen if the industry at last adopts standardized reactors and the Bush or a future administration streamlines the plant approval process.

Cutting Consumerism Is the Key

On a more fundamental level, any defeat of nuclear power is likely to be short-lived if America does not confront what Diamond calls its core value of consumerism. After all, there is only so much waste to wring out of any given economy. Eventually, if human population and appetites keep growing—and some growth is inevitable, given the ambitions of China and other newly industrializing nations—new sources of energy must be exploited. At that point, nuclear power and other undesirable alternatives such as shale oil will be waiting. (For the record, that is Brand's rejoinder future demand growth makes nuclear, as well as efficiency and renewables, necessary. Diamond did not respond to an e-mail request for comment.)

Environmentalists have been afraid to talk honestly about consumerism ever since a cardigan-clad Jimmy Carter was ridiculed for urging people to turn down their thermostats in the 1979 oil crisis. But now that our species, through our carbon-fueled pursuit of the good life, has turned up the planet's thermostat to ominous levels, it's time to break the silence. We don't have to freeze in the dark, but neither can we keep consuming as if there's no tomorrow.

| "Enough solar energy falls on the sur-
face of the Earth every forty minutes to
meet 100 percent of the entire world's
energy needs for a full year."

Renewable Energies Can Help Curb Global Warming

Matthew Rothschild

In the following viewpoint, Matthew Rothschild argues that the United States needs to move to carbon-free renewable energy in order to combat the effects of global warming. While oil and coal prices are going up, the prices of the most promising sources of renewable energy, such as solar, wind, and geothermal power, are becoming more affordable. Rothschild claims that investing in renewable energy has other benefits, such as stimulating the economy. Matthew Rothschild has been the editor of The Progressive *magazine since 1994.*

As you read, consider the following questions:

1. When do scientists predict that the Arctic Ocean will be totally ice free?

Matthew Rothschild, "Global Warming Challenge," *The Progressive*, vol. 72, September 2008, pp. 8–10. Copyright © 2008 by The Progressive, Inc. Reproduced by permission of *The Progressive*, 409 East Main Street, Madison, WI 53703, www.progressive.org.

2. What has "radically changed the economics of energy," according to Al Gore?

3. According to Al Gore, what is the greatest obstacle to meeting the challenge of 100 percent renewable electricity in ten years?

George Bush has committed so many criminal and derelict acts it's hard to figure out which ones are the worst of all. There's the Iraq War. There's the illegal spying on Americans. There's torture. There's kidnapping (I refuse to call it "extraordinary rendition"). There's the corruption of the Justice Department not only in its hirings but in its prosecutions. There's the outing of Valerie Plame, and the coverup. There's Katrina. And many more: Just glance at Dennis Kucinich's thirty-five articles of impeachment and you can get a sense of the magnitude of malfeasance.

But one issue may ultimately loom larger than all of these. And that's Bush's abysmal performance on global warming.

From beginning to end, his aggressive anti-intellectualism, his rich-kid arrogance, and his corporate allegiance have brought us the most backward and destructive policies imaginable—all at a time when foresight, not foolishness, was called for.

Let's review the tape.

He first denied the existence of global warming, and the human and corporate contributions to it.

Then he pulled us out of Kyoto.

Then his political appointees censored the scientists and edited, like some crazed Lysenko, the real science out of the policy papers.

He did nothing for six years about raising auto emissions standards, and then only reluctantly agreed to a change in the law that will raise fuel efficiency to 35 miles per gallon—by the year 2020!

He paid only lip service to solar and wind and other clean energies.

He did the same for conservation, which Cheney derided as a mere lifestyle choice. Bush and Cheney have just assumed that high demand was a given—and to put the blame on China and India if anyone complained.

For fiscal 2009, Bush proposed a 27 percent cut for energy efficiency programs and renewables.

Then, this spring [2008], when Democrats tried to get a bill on global warming finally through the Congress, the Bush Administration prevailed on Republican legislators to put the kibosh to it.

While Bush and Cheney fiddled, the planet's been burning.

In July [2008], two huge chunks of ice broke off the Canadian Arctic shelf. Scientists are predicting that the Arctic Ocean will be totally ice free during the summer of 2013.

Unusually powerful hurricanes, like Katrina and Rita, have kicked up, just as scientists predicted. So, too, did they predict the increasing number of tornadoes, the record heavy rains, the intense droughts, and the more frequent wildfires that we've been seeing.

It's likely to get worse.

If we don't take drastic action very soon, "hundreds of millions of people would become refugees" this century, NASA scientist James Hansen testified to Congress on June 23 [2008]. "Polar and alpine species will be pushed off the planet." Mountain glaciers will melt, lakes will dry up, and coral reefs will be destroyed, he predicted.

"We have already gone too far," said Hansen. "Time is running out."

So what does Bush do in his last visit to Europe at the G8 summit on global warming? He essentially gives the world the finger. After bollixing up any possibility of an agreement there, he took his final bow and said: "Goodbye from the world's biggest polluter."

What a guy!

Proposals to Reduce Global Warming

Fortunately, his successor is bound to be better. Barack Obama calls global warming "one of the greatest moral challenges of our generation." He has proposed reducing carbon emissions by 80 percent below 1990 levels by 2050. He wants to invest $150 billion in the next ten years in clean energy, and by 2025, he wants 25 percent of electricity consumed in the United to be "derived from clean, sustainable energy sources, like solar, wind, and geothermal," his website says. (He also is getting a lot of financial support from nuclear power companies, though his website is mum on nuclear.)

John McCain has long been one of the few Republicans to acknowledge global warming and to try to do something about it. He has drawn a sharp contrast between himself and Bush on this issue.

"I will not shirk the mantle of leadership that the United States bears," he said in a speech in Portland, Oregon, on May 12 [2008]. "I will not permit eight long years to pass without serious action on serious challenges."

On the nuts and bolts of policy, though, he wants to reduce carbon emissions only by 60 percent by 2050, and he is a huge proponent of nuclear power. He also believes that market-based solutions, like cap and trade, which Obama also supports, are the most important ones. But actually, if the government insisted on higher fuel efficiency standards for cars and trucks, and if the government spent money on subsidizing mass transit, and if the government poured money into solar and wind, that would do more than letting the private sector figure things out.

To be sure, Ralph Nader and Cynthia McKinney have better policy programs on global warming. Nader favors a carbon tax, opposes nuclear power, and stresses solar and wind energy. McKinney, the candidate of the Green Party, has called on the United States to become "carbon and nuclear free."

The Biofuel Potential

Fuels made from biomass (biofuels) offer a unique opportunity to reduce the net burden of CO_2 emissions to the atmosphere by providing a mechanism for photosynthetically recycling carbon from the tailpipes of cars and trucks back to biomass grown each year. Biofuels made from agricultural feedstocks (corn, agricultural residues, and energy crops) could save as much as 58 million metric tons per year of carbon (MtC) emissions by the year 2030. Biofuels have the added benefit of reducing U.S. reliance on foreign oil. In 2030 biofuels could supply 20% of the gasoline that was consumed in the United States in 2004.

John J. Sheehan,
"Potential Carbon Emissions Reductions
from Biofuels by 2030," in Charles F. Kutscher, ed.,
Tackling Climate Change in the U.S.,
Boulder, CO: American Solar Energy Society, January 2007.

More needs to be done than either Obama or McCain has proposed. Al Gore is once again showing the way on this issue. On July 17 [2008], he issued a challenge to the nation to produce "100 percent of our electricity from renewable energy and truly carbon-free sources within ten years. This goal is achievable, affordable, and transformative," he said. "It represents a challenge to all Americans, in every walk of life: to our political leaders, entrepreneurs, innovators, engineers, and to every citizen."

Gore said that the price of solar, wind, and geothermal power is going down and becoming affordable, just as the price of oil and coal is going out of sight. This has "radically changed the economics of energy," he said.

The potential for getting off of carbon-based fuels is abundant.

"Enough solar energy falls on the surface of the Earth every forty minutes to meet 100 percent of the entire world's energy needs for a full year," Gore said.

"Tapping just a small portion of this solar energy could provide all of the electricity America uses. And enough wind power blows through the Midwest corridor every day to also meet 100 percent of U.S. electricity demand."

Senator Bernie Sanders of Vermont has proposed one of the most forward-looking pieces of legislation to bring us down the path that Gore is blazing.

On July 7 [2008], he introduced a bill entitled the "10 Million Solar Roofs Act of 2008." It would require the Secretary of Energy to set up a program to provide rebates to individuals, businesses, and government buildings so they can put up solar panels on their roofs. Sanders's goal is to put up panels on ten million roofs in the next decade.

The rebate could account for up to "50 percent of the cost of the purchase and installation of the system," the bill says.

To qualify for the rebates, homeowners and businesses must demonstrate that they meet tough standards for energy efficiency.

In his bill, Sanders extols the promise of solar energy.

"There is a huge potential for increasing the quantity of electricity produced in the United States from distributed solar photovoltaics," it says. "The use of photovoltaics on the roofs of 10 percent of existing buildings could meet 70 percent of peak electric demand."

It would also be good for the economy.

"Investments in renewable energy stimulate the development of green jobs that provide substantial economic benefits," the bill states. Sanders is hopeful about this initiative. "We can reverse greenhouse gas emissions," he says. "We can break our dependence on foreign oil."

Challenges and Obstacles

But to pass Sanders's bill, much less to arrive at Gore's destination of a carbon-free grid, will require confronting corporate power. Gore himself pointed out the problem.

"The greatest obstacle to meeting the challenge of 100 percent renewable electricity in ten years may be the deep dysfunction of our politics and our self-governing system as it exists today," he said. "In recent years, our politics has tended toward incremental proposals made up of small policies designed to avoid offending special interests. . . . Our democracy has become sclerotic at a time when these crises require boldness."

James Hansen was even blunter. Testifying exactly twenty years after he first alerted Congress to the looming problem of global warming, Hansen said the "changes needed to preserve Creation, the planet on which civilization developed, are clear. But the changes have been blocked by special interests, focused on short-term profits, who hold sway in Washington and other capitals."

Placing the blame squarely on the shoulders of the fossil fuel companies, Hansen said they chose to "spread doubt about global warming, as tobacco companies discredited the smoking-cancer link."

He called the upcoming elections "critical for the planet," and he urged Americans to "turn out to pasture the most brontosaurian Congressmen."

But the problem that Hansen and Gore identify so well won't be solved simply by electing a few better members to Congress and a President who doesn't have his head in the sands of Saudi Arabia.

No, the problem won't be solved until we break the corporate stranglehold on our democracy. To do that, we need an organized, energized grassroots movement to use its power to overwhelm that of the ExxonMobils and the Halliburtons. And we need this movement to keep the pressure on Bush's successor so he doesn't backslide but moves forward toward the bold vision that Gore has offered.

Creating this movement may seem as difficult as transitioning off of oil and coal. But it need not be. There is a tremendous hunger, especially among young people, to take on the challenge of global warming. And there is a great urgency, among those of us in our later years, to attend to this problem before it's too late.

We all know who wields power in this country. It's the same group that has been polluting the Earth while it profits from fossil fuels.

We need to take its power away.

A reinvigorated green movement may end up not only saving the planet but saving our democracy, as well.

"Environmentally harmless increments of solar and renewable megawatts look puny in a 20 or 30 million megawatt world."

Renewable Energies Are Not a Practical Solution to Global Warming

Jesse H. Ausubel

Jesse H. Ausubel was the primary author of the 1983 report Changing Climate, *the first comprehensive assessment of the greenhouse effect. He is now a member of the Program for the Human Environment, a pro-environment research organization at Rockefeller University in New York. In the viewpoint that follows, Ausubel denies that renewable energy sources could have a profound effect on climate change or greenhouse gas emissions. According to Ausubel, resources such as hydro, wind, biomass, and solar power are costly and not environmentally friendly. More importantly, though, he contends that these energies are inefficient and could never supply the amount of power the world demands.*

Jesse H. Ausubel, "Renewable and Nuclear Heresies," *International Journal of Nuclear Governance, Economy and Ecology*, vol. 1, 2007, pp. 229–35. Copyright © 2007 Inderscience Enterprises Limited. All rights reserved. Reproduced by permission.

As you read, consider the following questions:

1. In Ausubel's estimation, how many square kilometers of land would a biomass-driven power plant need to supply the necessary fuel to produce 7.9 billion kilowatt hours?

2. What three disadvantages does Ausubel say plagues wind power as a viable renewable energy source?

3. What does Ausubel say is the general efficiency rating of most photovoltaic cells?

Heretics maintain opinions at variance with those generally received. Putting heretics to death, hereticide, is common through history. In 1531 the Swiss Protestant heretic Huldreich Zwingli soldiering anonymously in battle against the Catholic cantons was speared in the thigh and then clubbed on the head. Mortally wounded, he was offered the services of a priest. His declination caused him to be recognised, whereupon he was killed and quartered, and his body parts mixed with dung and ceremonially burned. Recall that the first heresy against the Roman Church in Switzerland in 1522 was the eating of sausages during Lent, and the signal heresy was opposition to the baptism of children. As nuclear experts know deeply, humans are not rational in their beliefs, actions or reactions.

I will offer both renewable and nuclear heresies. I trust readers will not commit hereticide. Because culture defines heresies, readers coming from a nuclear tribe will probably applaud my renewable heresies and grumble about the nuclear. While my heresies may not rival favouring polygamy or sharing all worldly goods, they will disturb many. My main heresies are that renewable sources of energy are not green and that the nuclear industry should make a product beside electricity. . . .

Hydropower: Too Much Space, Too Little Payoff

Let's consider the renewable idols: hydro, biomass, wind and solar. As a Green, I care intensely about land-sparing, about leaving land for Nature. In fact, a Green credo is 'No new structures'. Or, in milder form, 'New structures or infrastructures should fit within the footprint of the old structures or infrastructures'. So, I will examine renewables primarily by their use of land.

In the USA and much of the rest of the world, including Canada, renewables mean dammed rivers. Almost 80% of so-called US renewable energy is hydro, and hydro generates about 60% of all Canada's electricity.

For the USA as a whole, the capacity of all existing hydropower plants is about 97,500 MWe [megawatt electric], and their average production is about 37,500 MWe. The average power intensity—the watts divided by the land area of the USA—is 0.005 watts per square metre, that is, the approximate power that can be obtained from a huge tract of land that drains into a reservoir for a power station.

Imagine the entire province of Ontario, about 900,000 square km, collecting its entire 680,000 billion litres of rain, an average annual rainfall of about 0.8 m. Imagine collecting all that water, every drop, behind a dam of about 60 metres height. Doing so might inundate half the province, and thus win the support of the majority of Canadians, who resent the force of Ontario. This comprehensive 'Ontario Hydro' would produce about 11,000 MW or about four fifths the output of Canada's 25 nuclear power stations, or about 0.012 watts per square metre or more than twice the USA average. In my 'flood Ontario' scenario, a square kilometre would provide the electricity for about 12 Canadians.

This low density and the attending ecological and cultural headaches explain the trend in most of the world from dam building to dam removal. About 40% of Canada's immense total land area is effectively dammed for electrons already. The World Commission on Dams issued a report in November 2000 that essentially signalled the end of hydropower development globally. While the Chinese are constructing more dams, few foresee even ten thousand megawatts' further growth from hydropower.

Though electricity and hydrogen from hydro would decarbonise, the idol of hydro is itself dammed. Hydro is not green.

Biomass: Better Uses for Prime Land

In the USA, after hydro's 80% comes biomass's 17% of renewables. Surprisingly, most of this biomass comes, not from backyard woodsmen or community paper drives, but from liquors in pulp mills burned to economise their own heat and power. In terms of decarbonisation, biomass of course retrogresses, with 10 Cs [carbon atoms] or more per H [hydrogen].

If one argues that biomass is carbon-neutral because photosynthesis in plants recycles the carbon, one must consider its other attributes, beginning with productivity of photosynthesis. Although farmers usually express this productivity in tons per hectare, in the energy industry the heat content of the trees, corn and hay instead quantify the energy productivity of the land. For example, the abundant and untended New England or New Brunswick forests produce firewood at the renewable rate of about 1200 watts (thermal) per hectare averaged around the year. The 0.12 watts per square metre of biomass is about ten times more powerful than rain, and excellent management can multiply the figure again ten times.

Imagine, as energy analyst Howard Hayden has suggested, farmers use ample water, fertiliser, and pesticides to achieve 12,000 watts *thermal* per hectare (10,000 square metres). Imagine replacing a 1000 MWe nuclear power plant with a 90% capacity factor. During a year, the nuclear plant will produce about 7.9 billion kWh [kilowatt hours]. To obtain the same

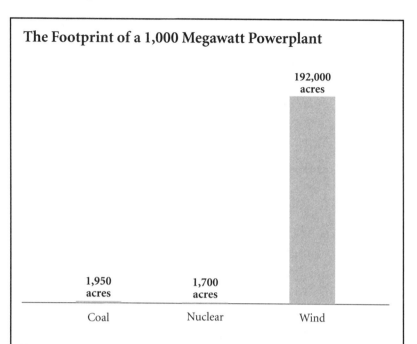

The Footprint of a 1,000 Megawatt Powerplant

192,000 acres

1,950 acres

1,700 acres

Coal   Nuclear   Wind

TAKEN FROM: H. Sterling Burnett, "Wind Power: Red Not Green," National Center for Policy Analysis, Brief Analysis No. 467, February 23, 2004.

electricity from a power plant that burns biomass at 30% heat-to-electricity efficiency, farmers would need about 250,000 hectares or 2500 square kilometres of land with very high productivity. Harvesting and collecting the biomass are not 100% efficient; some gets left in fields or otherwise lost.

Such losses mean that in round numbers a 1000 MWe nuclear plant equates to more than 2500 square kilometres of prime land. A typical Iowa county spans about 1000 square kilometres, so it would take at least two and a half counties to fire a station. A nuclear power plant consumes about ten hectares per unit or 40 hectares for a power park. Shifting entirely from bacon burgers to kilowatts, Iowa's 55,000 square miles might yield 50,000 MWe. Prince Edward Island might produce about 2000 MWe.

The USA already consumes about ten and the world about 40 times the kilowatt hours that Iowa's biomass could generate. Prime land has better uses, like feeding the hungry. Ploughing marginal lands would require ten or 20 times the expanse and increase erosion. One hundred twenty square metres of New Brunswick or Manitoba might electrify one square metre of New York City.

Note also that pumping water and making fertiliser and pesticides also consume energy. If processors concentrate the corn or other biomass into alcohol or diesel, another step erodes efficiency. Ethanol production yields a tiny net of 0.05 watts per square metre.

As in hydro, in biomass the lack of economies of scale loom large. Because more biomass quickly hits the ceiling of watts per square metre, it can become more extensive but not cheaper. If not false, the idol of biomass is not sustainable on the scale needed and will not contribute to decarbonisation. Biomass may photosynthesise but it is not green.

Wind: Temperamental and Inefficient

Although, or because, wind provides only 0.2% of US electricity, the idol of wind evokes much worship. The basic fact of wind is that it provides about 1.2 watts per square metre or 12,000 watts per hectare of year-round average electric power. Consider, for example, the $212 million wind farm about 30 kilometres south of Lamar, CO, where 108 1.5 MWe wind turbines stand 80 metres tall, their blades sweeping to 115 metres. The wind farm spreads over 4800 hectares. At 30% capacity, peak power density is the typical 1.2 watts per square metre.

One problem is that two of the four wind speed regimes produce no power at all. Calm air means no power of course, and gales faster than 25 metres per second (about 90 kilometres per hour) mean shutting down lest the turbine blow apart. Perhaps three to ten times more compact than biomass,

213

a wind farm occupying about 770 square kilometres could produce as much energy as one 1000 MWe nuclear plant. To meet 2005 US electricity demand of about four million MWhr with around-the-clock-wind would have required wind farms covering over 780,000 square kilometres, about Texas plus Louisiana, or about 1.2 times the area of Alberta. Canada's demand is about 10% of the USA and corresponds to about the area of New Brunswick.

For linear thinkers, a single file line of windmills has a power density of about 5 kilowatts per metre. If [environmentalist and artist] Christo could string windmills single file along Rocky Mountain ridges half way from Vancouver to Calgary, about 1200 km, the output would be about the same as one of the four Darlington CANDU [Canadian water reactors] units.

Rapidly exhausted economies of scale stop wind. One hundred windy square metres, a good size for a Manhattan apartment, can power a lamp or two, but not the clothes washer and dryer, microwave oven, plasma TVs or computers or dozens of other devices in the apartment, or the apartments above or below it. New York City would require every square metre of Connecticut to become a windfarm if the wind blew in Hartford as in Lamar. The idol of wind would decarbonise but will be minor.

Solar: Inefficient and Expensive

Although negligible as a source of electric power today, photovoltaics [PVs] also earn a traditional bow. Sadly, PVs remain stuck at about 10% efficiency, with no breakthroughs in 30 years. Today performance reaches about 5–6 watts per square metre. But no economies of scale inhere in PV systems. A 1000 MWe PV plant would require about 150 square kilometres plus land for storage and retrieval. Present USA electric consumption would require 150,000 square kilometres or a square almost 400 kilometres on each side. The PV industry now makes about 600 metres by 600 metres per year. About 600,000 times this amount would be needed to replace the 1000 MWe nuclear plant, but only a few square kilometres have ever been manufactured in total.

Viewed another way, to produce with solar cells the amount of energy generated in one litre of the core of a nuclear reactor requires one hectare of solar cells. To compete at making the millions of megawatts for the baseload of the world energy market, the cost and complication of solar collectors still need to shrink by orders of magnitude while efficiency soars.

Extrapolating the progress (or lack) in recent decades does not carry the solar and renewable system to market victory. Electrical batteries, crucial to many applications, weigh almost zero in the global energy market. Similarly, solar and renewable energy may attain marvellous niches, but seem puny for providing the base power for 8–10 billion people later this century.

The Damage Done

While I have denominated power with land so far, solar and renewables, despite their sacrosanct status, cost the environment in other ways as well. The appropriate description for PVs comes from the song of the Rolling Stones, 'Paint It Black'. Painting large areas with efficient, thus black, absorbers evokes dark 19th century visions of the land. I prefer colourful desert to a 150,000 km^2 area painted black. Some of the efficient PVs contain nasty elements, such as cadmium. Wind farms irritate with low-frequency noise and thumps, blight landscapes, interfere with TV reception, and chop birds and bats. At the Altamont windfarm in California, the mills kill 40–60 golden eagles per year. Dams kill rivers.

Moreover, solar and renewables in every form require large and complex machinery to produce many megawatts. Berkeley engineer Per Petersen reports that for an average MWe a typical wind-energy system operating with a 6.5 metres-per-second average wind speed requires construction inputs of 460 metric tons of steel and 870 cubic metres of concrete. For comparison, the construction of existing 1970-vintage US nuclear power plants required 40 metric tons of steel and 190 cubic metres of concrete per average megawatt of electricity generating capacity. Wind's infrastructure takes five to ten times the steel and concrete as that of nuclear. Bridging the cloudy and dark as well as calm and gusty weather takes storage batteries and their heavy metals. Without vastly improved storage, the windmills and PVs are supernumeraries for the coal, methane and uranium plants that operate reliably round the clock day after day.

Since 1980 the US DOE [Department of Energy] alone has spent about $6 billion on solar, $2 billion on geothermal, $1 billion on wind and $3 billion on other renewables. The nonhydro renewable energy remains about 2% of US capacity, much of that the wood byproducts used to fuel the wood products industry. Cheerful self-delusion about new solar and renewables since 1970 has yet to produce a single quad of the more than 90 quadrillion Btu [British thermal units] of the total energy the US now yearly consumes. In the 21 years from 1979 to 2000 the percentage of US energy from renewables actually fell from 8.5 to 7.3%. Environmentally harmless increments of solar and renewable megawatts look puny in a 20 or 30 million megawatt world, and even in today's 10 million megawatt world. If we want to scale up, then hydro, biomass, wind, and solar all gobble land from Nature. Let's stop sanctifying false and minor gods and heretically chant 'Renewables are not Green'.

| "Today, the movement against global warming . . . appears reticent to play political hard ball."

The Anti–Global Warming Movement Needs More Political Clout

Joel Bleifuss

In the viewpoint that follows, Joel Bleifuss argues that America's legislature is not sufficiently motivated to redress the problem of global warming. Instead, Bleifuss maintains that several congresspersons are actively stifling action on climate change issues because these senators and representatives are in the pay of fossil fuel–related industries. In Bleifuss's view, America needs a strong, politically motivated anti–global warming movement—on par with the Civil Rights Movement—to compel Congress to act and reduce carbon pollution. Joel Bleifuss is a journalist and the editor of In These Times, *a liberal newsmagazine.*

As you read, consider the following questions:

1. What does Bleifuss see as the weakness of the current anti–global warming movement?

Joel Bleifuss, "Global Warming: Dim Bulbs, Bright Lights," *In These Times*, April 13, 2007. Reproduced by permission of the publisher, www.inthesetimes.com.

2. As Bleifuss suggests, what actions *could* Congress take to drastically reduce the size of America's carbon footprint?

3. As Bleifuss writes, who has earned the nickname of "Tailpipe Johnny" and how did he acquire it?

People who want to save the Earth from the ravages of global warming face a perennial problem: How do they translate their concerns into actions that will create real change?

One barrier standing in the way of meaningful action is fuzzy-headed thinking on the part of those truly concerned about global warming. So worried are these activists, that their solution to the climate change problem is to marshal legions of Americans to change light bulbs, buy a Prius, or do any other number of helpful, but, in the big picture, not too significant feel-good actions.

For a full accounting of such a list go to the Alliance for Climate Protection Web site (www.allianceforclimateprotection .org), the nonprofit organization chaired by Al Gore. There you will learn: "What You Can Do," or more precisely, how your "own actions can also help reduce this threat." For example, the Web site advises:

Take Personal Action: You can reduce your personal contribution to global warming and set an example for others by using less gasoline, natural gas, oil, and electricity in your daily life. . . . Ask each member of your household to take responsibility for a different electricity-saving action. . . .

Encourage Community Action: . . . Encourage your local electric utilities to promote energy efficiency and the use of clean, renewable energy sources. . . .

Influence U.S. Action: The United States needs to play a leadership role in addressing global warming, and you can help make this happen. . . . Tell government officials that you want them to push industry to protect the future health of the environment by reducing carbon emissions.

Individual Actions Are Not Enough

These suggestions are all well and good. However, what is needed at this time of the global warming crisis is a movement that vigorously challenges the status quo, one that does more than advise citizens to "ask" members of their families to reduce energy use, or "encourage" electric utility corporations to be more efficient or, "tell" their elected representatives to "push" industry.

People, of course, should do what they can to reduce global warming. But they should never be made to think that their individual actions are the root cause of the problem or the ultimate solution.

Take the Civil Rights movement. Yes, personal reflection and individual change had its place, but can you imagine Martin Luther King telling people to "ask" their school boards to integrate the public schools, or "encourage" corporations not to discriminate, or "tell" their elected leaders to "push" legislatures in the South to do away with Jim Crow laws?

No. Political movements work when they mobilize a huge number of like-minded individuals and then use the ballot box to elect leaders who will change laws.

Forcing the Opposition to Act

Somehow, this is something progressives have long failed to understand. In the early '80s, the Freeze Movement galvanized the nation against the threat posed by the nuclear arms race, which at the time the [Ronald] Reagan administration was busy ratcheting up. However, because the movement was largely funded by 501(c)3 organizations that by law cannot get involved in electoral politics, the Freeze Movement concentrated on educating the public about the dangers of Mutually Assured Destruction (MAD) rather than mobilizing people to vote the Cold Warriors out of Congress.

Turn out the Brontosauruses

The fossil-industry maintains its strangle-hold on Washington via demagoguery, using China and other developing nations as scapegoats to rationalize inaction. In fact, we produced most of the excess carbon in the air today, and it is to our advantage as a nation to move smartly in developing ways to reduce emissions. As with the ozone problem, developing countries can be allowed limited extra time to reduce emissions. They will cooperate: they have much to lose from climate change and much to gain from clean air and reduced dependence on fossil fuels.

We must establish fair agreements with other countries. However, our own tax and dividend should start immediately. We have much to gain from it as a nation, and other countries will copy our success. . . .

Democracy works, but sometimes churns slowly. Time is short. The 2008 election is critical for the planet. If Americans turn out to pasture the most brontosaurian congressmen, if Washington adapts to address climate change, our children and grandchildren can still hold great expectations.

James Hansen,
"Global Warming Twenty Years Later: Tipping Points Near,"
briefing to the House Select Committee on Energy
Independence & Global Warming, June 23, 2008.

Similarly today, the movement against global warming, funded as it is by 501(c)3s like Gore's [nonprofit] outfit, appears reticent to play political hard ball.

The corporations that profit from the industrial processes that create global warming have no such compunction. They will never willingly sacrifice short-term profits for the long-term common good. And they well understand that Congress could force them to alter their behavior through a combination of legislative directives and economic incentives.

For example, Congress could require that all new vehicles sold in the United States meet minimum fuel efficiency and carbon emission standards by a set date, legislate that all new constructions projects be "green," or heavily invest in mass transit and reconstruct the national rail network. If lawmakers took such initiatives, the United States would drastically reduce the size of its carbon footprint.

Big Money Fights Back

Understandably, the industries that benefit from the status quo oppose such measures. To prevent change and the costs associated with it, corporations fund think tanks, hire PR [public relations] firms and pay lobbyists. They also fund the campaigns of those Representatives and Senators whose support they need to ensure no law passes that would adversely affect their industries. . . .

As legislative history bears out, the GOP [Republican Party] is underwritten by the industries culpable for global warming. Yet Democrats, while the favored recipients of support from environmental policy organizations, are not beyond the influence of big money.

In the House, a squabble has over about who will set the Democrats' climate change agenda. In January [2007], Speaker [Nancy] Pelosi established the House Select Committee on Energy Independence and Global Warming and named Rep. Ed Markey (D-Mass.), an environmentalist, as chair.

Whoops! This select committee did not sit too well with Rep. John Dingell (D-Mich.), who chairs the House Committee on Energy and Commerce. Dingell loves the auto industry, earning the moniker "Tailpipe Johnny" in the '80s for his opposition to legislation dealing with acid rain. Another unhappy camper, Rep. Rick Boucher (D-Va.), chairs the Subcommittee on Energy and Air Quality. He was concerned that the select committee might do something that would make his friends in the coal industry unhappy. According to the *Washington Post*, Boucher threatened to form an alliance with Republicans to block any legislation that Markey's committee would put forward.

Dingell, who has been in the House since 1955, and Boucher won a temporary reprieve when Pelosi gave them a deadline of June [2007] to come up with legislation to address global warming.

Don't hold your breath. According to data from the Center for Responsive Politics, since the 2000 election cycle, Dingell and Boucher have been the top Democratic recipients in the House of money from the "energy/natural resources" sector of the economy (the electric utilities, mining, and oil and gas industries), raking in $862,000 and $773,000 respectively.

And what can $1,635,000 buy on Capitol Hill? Inaction.

A Halt to Meaningful Action

[In 2006], Rep. Tom Udall (D-N.M.) introduced the Keep America Competitive Global Warming Policy Act of 2006, which sought to "establish a market-based system to regulate greenhouse gas emissions and to promote advanced energy research and technology development and deployment." In October [2006], Udall tried to get Dingell to look at his bill, but he would have none of it. As Dingell told the *Washington Post*, "If I thought it was a good idea, I would have already done it."

Boucher has a similar commitment to do-nothingism. On Nov. 28, 2005, he spoke at the Western Business Roundtable, Summit of the West. The American Coal Council Web site reported that Boucher and Pat Michaels, a senior fellow at the Cato Institute, told conference attendees "that the economic dislocation of policies such as Kyoto would ensure they would not achieve substantial greenhouse gas emissions reductions. Instead, they argued that voluntary actions with targeted incentives would accomplish more reductions and encourage the adoption of more efficient technologies." In other words, any meaningful action to address global warming was off the table.

On March 7 [2007], Boucher chaired a hearing titled, "Climate Change: Are Greenhouse Gas Emissions from Human Activities Contributing to a Warming of the Planet?" Gee, let's ponder the question—and then refer it to committee.

In the Senate, things look a little brighter with Sen. Barbara Boxer (D-Calif.) replacing Sen. James Inhofe (R-Okla.) as head of the Senate Committee on Environment and Public Works—though Inhofe has promised to filibuster any global "big lie" warming legislation that gets to the floor.

In short, while Congress is now in the hands of Democrats, that shift in power does not necessarily mean that vital issues like climate change will be adequately addressed. What's needed is a movement against global warming willing to play political hardball.

Yes, bless Gore for making the inconvenient truth about climate change part of the public dialogue. But if the new movement against global warming is going to get Congress to act, it will have to do more than pose an inconvenience to the likes of Dingell, Boucher and Inhofe. It will have to work to kick the bums out.

Periodical Bibliography

The following articles have been selected to supplement the diverse views presented in this chapter.

The Economist	"A Changing Climate of Opinion?" September 6, 2008.
Lynne Kiesling, Ronald Bailey, and Fred L. Smith	"Carbon: Tax, Trade, or Deregulate?" *Reason*, July 2008.
Robert Kunzig	"A Sunshade for Planet Earth," *Scientific American*, November 2008.
Bernice Lee	"Avoiding Climate Crunch," *World Today*, December 2008.
Mark Lynas	"Why the Greens Must Learn to Love Nuclear Power," *New Statesman*, September 22, 2008.
Jim Manzi	"And Global Warming Too!" *National Review*, January 26, 2009.
Bill McKibben	"The Green Back Effect," *Mother Jones*, May/June 2008.
Avery Palmer	"The Price of Being Green," *CQ Weekly*, October 6, 2008.
Sid Perkins	"Down with Carbon," *Science News*, May 10, 2008.
Richard J. Pierce Jr.	"Nuclear Energy Should—but Will Not—Be Part of an Effective Global Warming Mitigation Strategy," *Trends*, May/June 2008.
Alan Robock	"A Comment on . . . Geoengineering: It's Not a Panacea," *Geotimes*, July 2008.

For Further Discussion

Chapter 1

1. How does Ben Bova make his argument that global warming is a real phenomenon? What evidence does Edmund Contoski use to support his claim that global warming is unproven? Whose assertions do you find more convincing? Explain why.

2. Many observers agree with Michael Reagan that those who preach global warming make a considerable amount of money from their lectures and labors. After reading the viewpoints in this anthology, do you think that financial gain undercuts the message of those who wish to spread a warning about climate change? Explain why.

3. Brendan O'Neill maintains that the media are biased in their implicit support for those who believe in global warming. He insists that the American public should hear both sides of the argument so that they can make reasoned decisions on the issue. Do you agree with him that global warming deniers are unfairly sidelined by the media? How could this be corrected? Consider Joseph Romm's viewpoint in framing your answer.

Chapter 2

1. Both John W. Farley and Roy Spencer provide scientific evidence in their attempts to prove that global warming either is or is not the result of increases in human-produced carbon dioxide in the atmosphere. Does this use of scientific evidence lead you to believe these authors' arguments? Is one author more successful in his employ-

ment of scientific principles to prove that global warming is or is not caused by humans? Support your answer using evidence from the viewpoints.

2. Global warming deniers often accuse activists of using global warming to promote policies and behaviors that are driven by personal motives instead of a desire to curb climate change. Reread viewpoints 3–5 in this chapter and conduct some research into the authors' backgrounds. Do the authors' jobs or associations inform their viewpoints? Does this information change the way that you feel about a particular author's argument? Does an author's involvement with a particular organization or individual negate any of the facts that author may have espoused in his or her viewpoint? Explain your answers, referring to specific authors and viewpoints.

3. This chapter presents a variety of viewpoints claiming that particular factors have a key impact on global warming. First consider whether you find one of these viewpoints to be more convincing than the others. Explain why. If no viewpoint stands out as most convincing, explain why. Finally, decide whether you believe there is enough evidence for scientists and society at large to come to a consensus regarding the cause or causes of global warming. Explain your view.

Chapter 3

1. Jerome J. Schmitt argues that according to current estimates, global warming will not melt the polar ice caps or cause sea levels worldwide to rise. He uses scientific evidence and mathematic formulas to back up his views. Similarly, Lester R. Brown employs scientific evidence and formulas to support his view that the polar ice caps are melting; however, he also includes information regarding the consequences of the melting ice, such as decreased agricultural output and population displacement. Which

article did you find more convincing? Does this addition of potential, related consequences make Brown's article more persuasive?

2. In the debate over whether the polar bear is in fact threatened by global warming and melting ice caps, each side focuses on the amount and quality of evidence available. Those who believe the polar bear species should be protected, such as Kassie Siegel and Brendan Cummings, cite an abundance of evidence that polar bear populations are declining. Those who believe there is insufficient evidence, such as Kenneth P. Green, dissect the information and point out flaws and shortcomings. Reread the viewpoints and decide whether you believe sufficient evidence exists to connect global warming and polar bear population decline. Support your answer using information from both viewpoints.

3. Daniel J. Weiss and Robin Pam argue that mortality rates worldwide will increase as a result of global warming, adding that less developed countries will be most impacted. Bjorn Lomborg argues that global warming will actually serve to decrease mortality rates, contending that more deaths can be attributed to cold weather than hot weather, thus warmer weather will result in a decrease in cold weather deaths. Which argument do you agree with? Explain why, using quotations from the articles.

Chapter 4

1. Some environmentalists contend that President Barack Obama's support for a cap-and-trade emissions program will not go far enough to cut America's contribution to climate change. Read the viewpoints on the cap-and-trade/carbon tax proposals in this chapter and then do some extra research online or in magazines to find out more about these potential solutions. From your readings, explain whether you believe a cap-and-trade system is the

better choice for dealing with carbon emissions in these early years of the twenty-first century or if a straight carbon tax would be the wiser course of action.

2. In an introduction to their viewpoint, Matt Bennett, Rob Keast, and John Dyson state that "there does not seem to be a realistic path to resolving climate change that does not significantly expand nuclear energy." Explain why these authors hold this view. Then examine Mark Hertsgaard's line of reasoning and explain why he believes nuclear energy should not be part of the solution to global warming. Finally, explain where you think nuclear energy should fit—if at all—in America's future energy plan.

3. What kind of rhetorical strategies does Matthew Rothschilde use to make his case that America should pursue alternative energies to combat global warming? How does Jesse H. Ausubel's rhetorical technique differ from that of Rothschilde? Explain which argument you find more convincing and state whether the rhetorical devices the author used helped persuade you to side with his viewpoint.

Organizations to Contact

The editors have compiled the following list of organizations concerned with the issues debated in this book. The descriptions are derived from materials provided by the organizations. All have publications or information available for interested readers. The list was compiled on the date of publication of the present volume; the information provided here may change. Be aware that many organizations take several weeks or longer to respond to inquiries, so allow as much time as possible.

American Enterprise Institute (AEI)
1150 Seventeenth St. NW, Washington, DC   20036
(202) 862-5800 • fax: (202) 862-7177
Web site: www.aei.org

AEI is a public policy institute seeking to preserve and promote conservative values and public policy. The institute advocates for a government environmental policy that provides adequate protection for the environment without infringing on democratic institutions or human liberty. AEI dedicates a section of its Web site to publishing recent articles questioning the statement that "the science is settled" with regards to climate change. Additionally, articles critiquing current environmental policy are posted.

Cato Institute
1000 Massachusetts Ave. NW, Washington, DC   20001-5403
(202) 842-0200 • fax: (202) 842-3490
Web site: www.cato.org

The Cato Institute is an organization dedicated to espousing the libertarian principles of free market economics and limited government intervention in all areas of life. As such, Cato promotes energy and environmental policy that discourages government policies and incentives to push the development of sustainable energy sources, instead advocating for the free market's ability to provide the best solutions to environmental issues such as global warming. The institute worries that government intervention to protect the environment will only stifle economic liberty. Current articles and studies by Cato concerning global warming include "What to Do about Climate Change," "Is the Sky Really Falling? A Review of Recent Global Warming Scare Stories," and "Shaky Science: Inconvenient Truths Ignored by EPA in Its Proposal to Regulate Carbon Dioxide Emissions." These and others are available online.

Center for American Progress (CAP)

1333 H St. NW, 10th Floor, Washington, DC   20005
(202) 682-1611 • fax: (202) 682-1867
e-mail: progress@americanprogress.org
Web site: www.americanprogress.org

CAP is a progressive public policy institute that seeks to promote liberal values and point out the flaws of conservative government while encouraging the media to honestly present, analyze, and critique important current issues. CAP advocates for government policy that protects the environment by encouraging the development of sustainable energy technologies and reduces global dependence on carbon producing energy sources. Print and multimedia publications about global warming issues can be accessed on CAP's Web site.

Center for the Study of Carbon Dioxide and Global Change

PO Box 25697, Tempe, AZ   85285-5697
(480) 966-3719
Web site: www.co2science.org

The Center for the Study of Carbon Dioxide and Global Change seeks to be a voice of scientific reason to counter what it dubs "alarmist global warming propaganda." The center provides scientific analysis of the rising levels of atmospheric carbon dioxide (CO_2) in its weekly online magazine, *CO2 Science*. Additionally, the organization posts online instructions for experiments that individuals can conduct in the classroom or at home to personally assess CO2 enrichment and depletion.

Climate Institute

900 Seventeenth St. NW, Suite 700, Washington, DC   20006
(202) 547-0104 • fax: (202) 547-0111
e-mail: info@climate.org
Web site: www.climate.org

The Climate Institute is a nonprofit organization with the goals of identifying methods of reducing environmentally harmful emissions and informing both the public and policy makers about current options to halt global climate change. The organization attempts to maintain a reliable, unbiased source of information on global warming. Specific topics addressed by the institute with regard to climate change include sea level rise, changes in weather patterns, the impact on human health, and ozone depletion. Publications on these issues and others can be read online.

Competitive Enterprise Institute (CEI)

1899 L St. NW, 12th Floor, Washington, DC   20036
(202) 331-1010 • fax: (202) 331-0640
email: info@cei.org
Web site: www.cei.org

CEI is a public policy think tank dedicated to promoting the ideals of the free market system. Additionally, the institute advocates for limited government regulation. With regards to environmental policy, CEI believes the free market will provide the ideas and ingenuity to solve environmental problems and that government regulation only stifles progressive action. GlobalWarming.org is a Web site maintained by CEI, providing arguments and research to support claims that the problems associated with global climate change have been overstated and exaggerated. Publications by the organization can be found on this Web site and the CEI home page.

Earth Policy Institute (EPI)

1350 Connecticut Ave. NW, Suite 403, Washington, DC   20036
(202) 496-9290 • fax: (202) 496-9325
e-mail: epi@earthpolicy.org
Web site: www.earthpolicy.org

Since its founding in 2001, EPI has sought to inform individuals worldwide about the problems presented by global climate change and to provide viable solutions for a sustainable future. EPI employs the Internet, mass communications media, and book publication to get its message out to the public. PDFs of many of the organization's publications are available online.

Food and Agriculture Organization of the United Nations (FAO)

Viale delle Terme di Caracalla, Rome   00153
   Italy
(+39) 06 57051 • fax: (+39) 06 570 53152
Web site: www.fao.org

Within the United Nations, FAO is the department in charge of addressing agricultural- and food-related issues. Environment, climate change, and bioenergy is one division within this larger organizational structure. While the office's main goal is to eradicate hunger worldwide, global warming plays a significant role in the production of food agriculture products, especially in developing nations. Specifically, FAO examines the ways in which climate change will affect already vulnerable populations and their food sources. Publications and information about current efforts can be found on the organization's Web site.

Heritage Foundation

214 Massachusetts Ave. NE, Washington, DC   20002-4999
(202) 546-4400 • fax: (202) 546-8328
e-mail: info@heritage.org
Web site: www.heritage.org

A conservative public policy institute, Heritage contends that government policy implemented to curb global warming will have severe economic impacts on the United States and its citizens. Recent commentaries on global warming–related issues include "CO2 Emission Cuts: The Economic Costs of the EPA's ANPR Regulations," "'A Glorious Mess': EPA Notice Would Have Dramatic Impact on U.S. Military," and "EPA Should Not Ignore Congress on Global Warming Restrictions." These publications and others can be accessed on the Heritage Web site.

Pew Center on Global Climate Change
2101 Wilson Blvd., Suite 550, Arlington, VA   22201
(703) 516-4146 • fax: (703) 841-1422
Web site: www.pewclimate.org

The Pew Center on Global Climate Change seeks the cooperation of those working in private industry, government, and scientific fields to address the issues of global warming using science, honesty, and integrity. The center funds research and publications, works directly with policy makers and business leaders to find feasible solutions to climate change problems, and educates the public about their role in slowing global warming. The organization's Web site provides access to publications on topics ranging from the basics of global warming to scientific and economic impact to technological solutions.

United States Environmental Protection Agency (EPA)
Ariel Rios Building, 1200 Pennsylvania Ave. NW
Washington, DC   20460
(202) 272-0167
Web site: www.epa.gov

The EPA is the U.S. government agency charged with protecting the environment and the health of U.S. citizens by developing and enforcing environmental regulations, grant-giving, conducting research and publishing studies, and working in partnership with non-governmental organizations. Additionally, the EPA seeks to educate the U.S. public about current environmental issues. The EPA climate change Web site, www.epa.gov/climatechange, provides the latest information on global warming–related topics such as greenhouse gas emissions, U.S. climate change policy, health and environmental effects, and actions individuals can take to slow global warming. Reports published by the EPA can be accessed online.

World Health Organization (WHO)
Avenue Appia 20, Geneva 27   1211
  Switzerland
(+41) 22-791-2111 • fax: (+41) 22-791-3111
e-mail: info@who.int
Web site: www.who.int

WHO is the office within the United Nations (UN) dedicated to improving the health of populations worldwide by providing international direction on global health issues, dictating the UN health research priorities, assisting countries with their health problems, and establishing a set of norms and standards for health. With regards to climate change, this organization focuses on analyzing the ways in which global warming will impact human health in both the short and long term. Topics considered include changes in cases of infectious disease, changes to food production and agriculture, and occurrences of extreme weather events. Reports and background information can be read on the WHO Web site.

Bibliography of Books

William James Burroughs	*Climate Change: A Multidisciplinary Approach.* New York: Cambridge University Press, 2007.
Paul K. Conkin	*The State of the Earth: Environmental Challenges on the Road to 2100.* Lexington, KY: University of Kentucky Press, 2007.
Andrew E. Dessler and Edward A. Parson	*The Science and Politics of Global Climate Change: A Guide to the Debate.* New York: Cambridge University Press, January 23, 2006.
Joseph F.C. DiMento and Pamela Doughman, eds.	*Climate Change: What It Means for Us, Our Children, and Our Grandchildren.* Cambridge, MA: MIT Press, 2007.
Kerry Emanuel	*What We Know About Climate Change.* Cambridge, MA: MIT Press, 2007.
Thomas L. Friedman	*Hot, Flat, and Crowded: Why We Need a Green Revolution—and How It Can Renew America.* New York: Farrar, Straus and Giroux, 2008.
James Garvey	*The Ethics of Climate Change: Right and Wrong in a Warming World.* New York: Continuum, 2008.

Indur M. Goklany   *The Improving State of the World:*
                   Why We're Living Longer, Healthier,
                   More Comfortable Lives on a Cleaner
                   Planet. Washington, DC: Cato
                   Institute, 2007.

Al Gore   *An Inconvenient Truth: The Crisis of*
                   Global Warming. New York: Viking,
                   2007.

Christopher C.   *Red Hot Lies: How Global Warming*
Horner   *Alarmists Use Threats, Fraud, and*
                   Deception to Keep You Misinformed.
                   Washington, DC: Regnery, 2008.

Judith A. Layzer   *The Environmental Case: Translating*
                   Values Into Policy. Washington, DC:
                   CQ Press, 2006.

P.H. Liotta and   *Gaia's Revenge: Climate Change and*
Allan W. Shearer   *Humanity's Loss.* Westport, CT:
                   Praeger, 2007.

Bjorn Lomborg   *Cool It: The Skeptical*
                   Environmentalist's Guide to Global
                   Warming. New York: Vintage Books,
                   2008.

Patrick J.   *Shattered Consensus: The True State of*
Michaels   *Global Warming.* Lanham, MD:
                   Rowman & Littlefield, 2005.

Peter Newman,   *Resilient Cities: Responding to Peak*
Timothy Beatley,   *Oil and Climate Change.* Washington,
and Heather   DC: Island, 2009.
Boyer

David Shearman and Joseph Wayne Smith — *The Climate Change Challenge and the Failure of Democracy.* Westport, CT: Praeger, 2007.

Lawrence Solomon — *The Deniers: The World Renowned Scientists Who Stood Up Against Global Warming Hysteria, Political Persecution, and Fraud—And Those Who Are too Fearful to Do So.* Minneapolis, MN: Richard Vigilante, 2008.

Roy Spencer — *Climate Confusion: How Global Warming Hysteria Leads to Bad Science, Pandering Politicians and Misguided Policies that Hurt the Poor.* New York: Encounter, 2008.

Robert G. Strom — *Hot House: Global Climate Change and the Human Condition.* New York: Copernicus, 2007.

Mike Tidwell — *The Ravaging Tide: Strange Weather, Future Katrinas, and the Coming Death of America's Coastal Cities.* New York: Free Press, 2006.

Gabrielle Walker and Sir David King — *The Hot Topic: What We Can Do about Global Warming.* Orlando, FL: Harcourt, 2008.

Peter Douglas Ward — *Under a Green Sky: Global Warming, the Mass Extinctions of the Past, and What They Mean for Our Future.* New York: Smithsonian, 2007.

Index